2014

中国国际收支报告
China's Balance of Payments Report

国家外汇管理局国际收支分析小组
BOP Analysis Group
State Administration of Foreign Exchange

中国金融出版社
China Financial Publishing House

责任编辑：张翠华
责任校对：孙　蕊
责任印制：裴　刚

图书在版编目（CIP）数据

2014 中国国际收支报告（2014 Zhongguo Guoji Shouzhi Baogao）／国家外汇管理局国际收支分析小组 ． —北京：中国金融出版社，2015.7

　ISBN 978-7-5049-8061-8

　Ⅰ．① 2··· 　Ⅱ．①国··· 　Ⅲ．①国际收支—研究报告—中国—2014
Ⅳ．① F812.4

　中国版本图书馆 CIP 数据核字（2015）第 169023 号

出版
发行　**中国金融出版社**

社址　北京市丰台区益泽路 2 号
市场开发部　　（010）63266347，63805472，63439533　（传真）
网上书店　http://www.chinafph.com　　（010）63286832，63365686　（传真）
读者服务部　（010）66070833，62568380
邮编　100071
经销　新华书店
印刷　天津银博印刷有限公司
尺寸　210 毫米 × 285 毫米
印张　12.75
字数　195 千
版次　2015 年 7 月第 1 版
印次　2015 年 7 月第 1 次印刷
印数　1—2000
定价　80.00 元
ISBN 978-7-5049-8061-8/F.7621
如出现印装错误本社负责调换　联系电话：（010）63263947

《中国国际收支报告》（2014年）分析小组人员名单

组　　长：易　纲

副组长：邓先宏　方上浦　王小奕　李　超　杨国中　韩红梅

审　　稿：王允贵　杜　鹏　郭　松　张生会　王春英　崔汉忠

统　　稿：管　涛　方　文　温建东　周　济　赵玉超

执　　笔：

第一部分：管恩杰　李　伟　高　铮

第二部分：高　峰　杨　灿　查晓阳　李玲青　马玉娟

第三部分：胡　红

第四部分：贾　宁　梁　艳

第五部分：马　昀

专　　栏：周　济　吕　晓　乔林智　夏座蓉　段　盈

附录整理：李　伟

英文翻译：周海文　王　亮　胡　红

英文审校：Nancy Hearst（美国哈佛大学费正清东亚研究中心）

Contributors to This Report

Head
Yi Gang

Deputy Head
Deng Xianhong   Fang Shangpu   Wang Xiaoyi   Li Chao
Yang Guozhong   Han Hongmei

Readers
Wang Yungui   Du Peng   Guo Song   Zhang Shenghui
Wang Chunying   Cui Hanzhong

Editors
Guan Tao   Fang Wen   Wen Jiandong   Zhou Ji   Zhao Yuchao

Authors
Part One: Guan Enjie   Li Wei   Gao Zheng
Part Two: Gao Feng   Yang Can   Zha Xiaoyang   Li Lingqing
Ma Yujuan
Part Three: Hu Hong
Part Four: Jia Ning   Liang Yan
Part Five: Ma Yun
Boxes: Zhou Ji   Lv Xiao   Qiao Linzhi   Xia Zuorong   Duan Ying

Appendix: Li Wei

Translators: Zhou Haiwen   Wang Liang   Hu Hong

Proofreader: Nancy Hearst (Fairbank Center for East Asian Research,
Harvard University)

内容摘要

2014 年，全球经济延续缓慢复苏态势，各国经济运行和货币政策取向出现分化，国际金融市场波动加大。我国经济运行处于合理区间，改革和结构调整稳步推进，人民币汇率双向浮动明显增强。

2014 年，我国国际收支在震荡中趋向基本平衡。经常项目顺差 2 197 亿美元，较上年增长 48%，与 GDP 之比为 2.1%，仍处于国际公认的合理水平之内。其中，货物贸易顺差增长 32%，服务贸易逆差扩大 54%。同时，跨境资本流动的波动性明显增强。第一季度延续了 2013 年底的净流入态势，资本和金融项目顺差 940 亿美元。第二季度以来，受国内外经济金融环境变化、人民币汇率双向波动等因素共同影响，资本和金融项目转为逆差，第二季度至第四季度累计逆差 557 亿美元。具体来看，直接投资持续较大规模净流入；证券投资、其他投资等非直接投资形式的跨境资本由净流入转为净流出，主要体现了境内主体持汇意愿增强和对外偿债加快。2014 年，我国新增储备资产 1 178 亿美元，较上年下降 73%，相当于国内生产总值的 1.1%，较上年回落 3.4 个百分点。

2015 年，预计我国国际收支仍将保持"经常项目顺差、资本和金融项目双向波动"的格局。外汇管理部门将主动适应国际收支形势的新常态，以促进国际收支平衡为目标、以防范跨境资本冲击为前提，继续促进贸易投资便利化，积极推动外汇市场发展，稳步推进人民币资本项目可兑换等关键改革，加快构建宏观审慎管理框架下的外债和资本流动管理体系，完善外汇储备经营管理。

Abstract

In 2014 the global economy continued to recover slowly, with differentiated economic performance and monetary policies in various countries and surging fluctuation in international financial markets. The Chinese economy grew at a reasonable rate. The government steadily promoted reform and structural adjustments, and the RMB exchange rate experienced more significant two–way fluctuations.

China's balance of payments was moving in a generally balanced direction amidst fluctuations. The current account surplus totaled USD 219.7 billion, up by 48 percent year on year. The ratio of the current account surplus to GDP was 2.1 percent, which by international standards was considered reasonable. In particular, the trade in goods surplus grew by 32 percent whereas the trade in services deficit increased by 54 percent. In the meantime, cross–border capital flows fluctuated significantly. As in 2013 the first quarter continued to record net inflows, with the surplus totaling USD 94 billion. However, the capital and financial account recorded a deficit in the following three quarters, with a total deficit of USD 55.7 billion due to the changing economic and financial situations both domestically and internationally and the two–way floating RMB exchange rate since the second quarter. More specifically, direct investments continued to record net inflows whereas non–direct investments, such as portfolio investments and other investments, changed from net inflows to net outflows, driven by the strengthened willingness to hold foreign exchange and the increase in repayment of the external debt. In 2014 China's reserve assets increased by USD 117.8 billion, down by 73 percent year on year, which accounted for 1.1 percent of GDP, 3.4 percentage points lower than the ratio in 2013.

In 2015 China's balance of payments are projected to maintain a surplus in the current account and two–way fluctuations in the capital and financial account. The SAFE will actively adapt to the new normal of the balance of payments, promote trade and investment facilitation and foreign exchange market development, propel key reforms for capital account convertibility, construct an external debt and capital flow management system in the context of macro prudential management, and improve foreign reserve management with the goal of achieving a general BOP balance and guarding against shocks from cross–border capital flows.

目 录

专栏

图

表

Contents

Boxes

Charts

Table

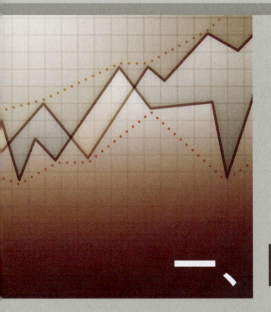

一、国际收支概况

（一）国际收支运行环境

2014 年，我国面临的国际国内环境复杂严峻，全球经济曲折复苏，国内经济保持在合理区间运行但下行压力有所增加，人民币汇率双向浮动弹性明显增强，我国国际收支在震荡中趋向基本平衡。

从国际看，2014 年世界经济延续不平衡的缓慢复苏，各经济体经济运行存在差异（见图 1-1），货币政策走势分化。美国经济先抑后扬，总体增长势头较为强劲，就业市场状况继续改善，美联储逐步缩减购债规模，并于 10 月结束量化宽松货币政策；欧元区受通货紧缩和高失业率等负面因素困扰，经济增长依然低位徘徊，日本经济自第二季度开始连续三个季度陷入负增长，欧元区和日本宽松货币政策力度进一步加大；部分新兴经济体面临内生增长动力不足、资产价格下跌甚至资本外流等多重困难，在刺激经济与限制资本外流之间抉择各自的货币政策。复杂的货币政策与低增长的全球经济交织，加大国际金融市场波动。一方面，主要股票和债券市场总体上行，下半年震荡加大；另一方面，美元展开一轮趋势性升值，非美货币和大宗商品价格普遍下挫（见图 1-2）。

图 1-1

2007-2014 年主要经济体和国家季度经济增长率

注：美国数据为季度环比折年率，其他经济体数据为季度同比。
数据来源：环亚经济数据库。

图 1-2

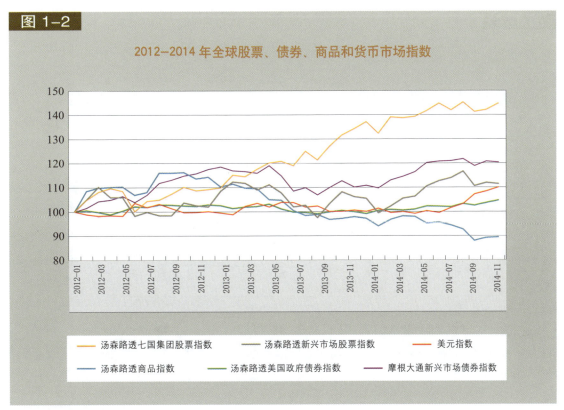

2012—2014 年全球股票、债券、商品和货币市场指数

图例：
- 汤森路透七国集团股票指数
- 汤森路透新兴市场股票指数
- 美元指数
- 汤森路透商品指数
- 汤森路透美国政府债券指数
- 摩根大通新兴市场债券指数

注：2012 年初值为 100。
数据来源：路透数据库。

图 1-3

2008—2014 年我国季度 GDP 和月度 CPI 增长率

图例：
- 季度 GDP 同比增长率（左轴）
- 月度 CPI 同比增长率（右轴）

数据来源：环亚经济数据库。

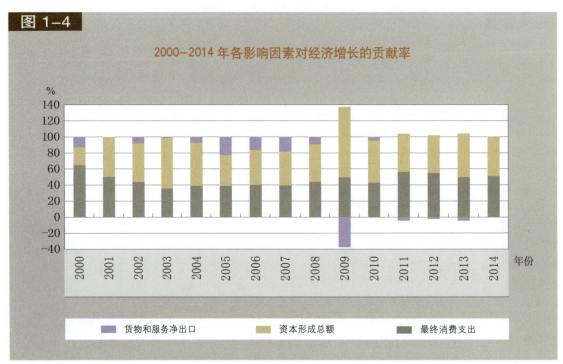

图 1-4

2000—2014 年各影响因素对经济增长的贡献率

图例：货物和服务净出口　资本形成总额　最终消费支出

数据来源：环亚经济数据库。

从国内看，2014 年我国经济社会发展总体平稳、稳中有进，但前进中也面临诸多困难和挑战。从积极因素看，国内生产总值保持了中高速增长，居民消费价格涨幅较低（见图 1-3），就业市场总体稳定；产业结构更趋优化，最终消费支出对经济增长的拉动加大（见图 1-4）；人民币汇率双向浮动区间扩大，汇率弹性增加，对国际收支的价格调节作用进一步发挥。从不利因素看，投资增长乏力，新的消费热点不多，稳增长难度加大，"三期"叠加背景下一些领域仍存在风险隐患，加速了市场主体资产负债币种结构的调整。

（二）国际收支主要状况

国际收支呈现"双顺差"。2014 年，我国国际收支总顺差 2 579 亿美元，较 2013 年 [①] 下降 48%（见表 1-1）。其中，经常项目顺差 2 197 亿美元，增长 48%；资本和金融项目顺差 382 亿美元，下降 89%。

---

① 2013 年国际收支平衡表已根据最新获得的数据进行修订。修订后，2013 年国际收支总顺差 4 943 亿美元。其中，经常项目顺差 1 482 亿美元，调减了 346 亿美元，资本和金融项目顺差 3 461 亿美元，调增了 199 亿美元。主要是按外商投资企业年检实际数调整了外来直接投资未分配利润和已分配未汇出利润，令全年收益流出和外国来华直接投资流入各调增 354 亿美元。

　　货物贸易顺差增长较快。按国际收支统计口径^①，2014 年，我国货物贸易出口 23 541 亿美元，进口 18 782 亿美元，分别较上年增长 6% 和 1% ；顺差 4 760 亿美元，增长 32%（见图 1-5）。

表 1-1　2008-2014 年中国国际收支顺差结构　　　　　　　　　　　　　　　　　单位：亿美元，%

项　目	2008 年	2009 年	2010 年	2011 年	2012 年	2013 年	2014 年
国际收支总差额	4 607	4 417	5 247	4 016	1 836	4 943	2 579
经常项目差额	4 206	2 433	2 378	1 361	2 154	1 482	2 197
占国际收支总差额比重	91	55	45	34	117	30	85
与 GDP 之比	9.3	4.9	4.0	1.9	2.6	1.6	2.1
资本和金融项目差额	401	1 985	2 869	2 655	−318	3 461	382
占国际收支总差额比重	9	45	55	66	−17	70	15
与 GDP 之比	0.9	4.0	4.8	3.6	−0.4	3.6	0.4

数据来源：国家外汇管理局、国家统计局。

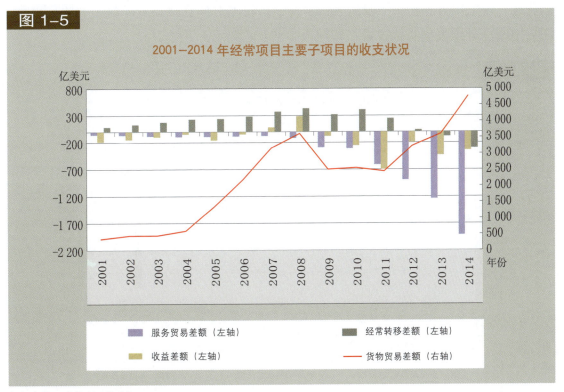

图 1-5

2001-2014 年经常项目主要子项目的收支状况

数据来源：国家外汇管理局。

　　　　———————————

　　① 本口径与海关口径的主要差异在于，一是海关统计的到岸价进口额按 5% 减去其中的运输和保险费用后计为国际收支口径的进口；二是国际收支口径还包括货物修理、运输工具在港口购买的货物以及抓获的进出口走私，并分别在进出口中扣除了退货。

服务贸易逆差继续扩大。2014年，服务贸易收入1 909亿美元，较上年下降7%；支出3 829亿美元，增长16%；逆差1 920亿美元，扩大54%，其中，运输项目逆差较上年微增2%，旅游项目逆差延续扩大态势，增长40%（见图1–5）。

收益项目逆差收窄。2014年，收益项目收入2 130亿美元，较上年增长16%；支出2 471亿美元，下降6%；逆差341亿美元，缩小57%。其中，职工报酬顺差258亿美元，扩大60%；投资收益逆差599亿美元，下降37%（见图1–5）。投资收益为负，不代表我国对外投资损失，实际上，当年我国对外投资收益1 831亿美元，较上年增长10%；外来投资利润利息、股息红利支出2 429亿美元，较上年下降7%。

经常转移逆差大幅增长。2014年，经常转移收入411亿美元，较上年下降23%；支出714亿美元，增长15%；逆差302亿美元，增长2.5倍（见图1–5）。经常转移主要包括捐赠、赔偿、社会保障、税收、罚款以及博彩等。自2013年起，经常转移由顺差转为逆差，反映了随着居民收入提高，境内对境外的捐赠增多。

直接投资净流入小幅下降。按国际收支统计口径，2014年，直接投资顺差2 087亿美元，较上年下降4%（见图1–6）。其中，我国对外直接投资净流出804亿美元，增长10%；外国来华直接投资<u>①</u>净流入2 891亿美元，下降1%。

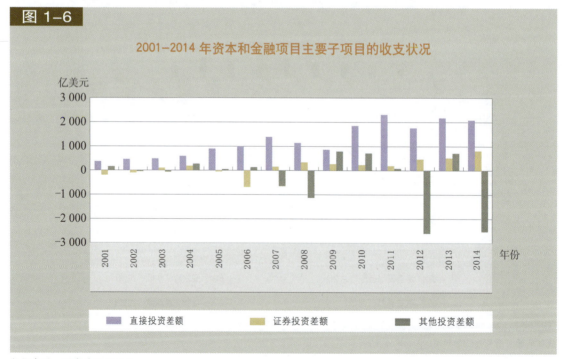

图1–6

2001–2014年资本和金融项目主要子项目的收支状况

亿美元

（图例：直接投资差额　证券投资差额　其他投资差额）

数据来源：国家外汇管理局。

———————

① 本口径与商务部公布的数据主要差异在于，国际收支统计中还包括了外商投资企业的未分配利润、已分配未汇出利润、盈余公积、股东贷款、金融机构吸收外资、非居民购买不动产等内容。

图 1-7

2001-2014 年外汇储备增加额与外汇储备余额

注：图中外汇储备增加额为交易引起的变化，剔除了估值效应的影响。
数据来源：国家外汇管理局。

证券投资净流入快速增长。 2014 年，证券投资项下净流入 824 亿美元，较上年增长 56%（见图 1-6）。其中，我国对外证券投资净流出 108 亿美元，扩大 102%；境外对我国证券投资净流入 932 亿美元，增长 60%。

其他投资由净流入转为净流出。 2014 年，其他投资项下净流出 2 528 亿美元，而上年为净流入 722 亿美元（见图 1-6）。其中，我国对外的贷款、贸易信贷和资金存放等资产净增加 3 030 亿美元，较上年增长 113%；境外对我国的贷款、贸易信贷和资金存放等负债净增加 502 亿美元，下降 77%。

储备资产增幅放缓。 2014 年，我国新增储备资产（剔除汇率、价格等非交易价值变动影响，下同）1 178 亿美元，较上年下降 73%，其中，外汇储备资产增加 1 188 亿美元，下降 73%。截至 2014 年末，我国外汇储备余额达 38 430 亿美元（见图 1-7），较上年末增加 217 亿美元，同比少增 4 880 亿美元。外汇储备余额增幅小于外汇储备资产 971 亿美元，主要反映了国际市场上主要货币汇率和资产价格变化带来账面估值的波动，并没有实际的跨境资金流动。

表 1-2 2014 年中国国际收支平衡表 [①]

单位：亿美元

项　　目	差　额	贷　方	借　方
一、经常项目	**2 197**	**27 992**	**25 795**
A．货物和服务	2 840	25 451	22 611
a．货物	4 760	23 541	18 782
b．服务	−1 920	1 909	3 829
1．运输	−579	382	962
2．旅游	−1 079	569	1 649
3．通讯服务	−5	18	23
4．建筑服务	105	154	49
5．保险服务	−179	46	225
6．金融服务	−4	45	49
7．计算机和信息服务	99	184	85
8．专有权利使用费和特许费	−219	7	226
9．咨询	164	429	265
10．广告、宣传	12	50	38
11．电影、音像	−7	2	9
12．其他商业服务	−217	14	231
13．别处未提及的政府服务	−10	11	20
B．收益	−341	2 130	2 471
1．职工报酬	258	299	42
2．投资收益	−599	1 831	2 429
C．经常转移	−302	411	714
1．各级政府	−29	16	46
2．其他部门	−273	395	668
二、资本和金融项目	**382**	**25 730**	**25 347**
A．资本项目	0	19	20
B．金融项目	383	25 710	25 328
1．直接投资	2 087	4 352	2 266
1.1 我国在外直接投资	−804	555	1 359
1.2 外国在华直接投资	2 891	3 797	906
2．证券投资	824	1 664	840
2.1 资产	−108	293	401
2.1.1 股本证券	−14	170	184
2.1.2 债务证券	−94	123	217
2.1.2.1（中）长期债券	−92	123	215
2.1.2.2 货币市场工具	−2	0	2
2.2 负债	932	1 371	439
2.2.1 股本证券	519	777	258
2.2.2 债务证券	413	594	181
2.2.2.1（中）长期债券	410	497	88
2.2.2.2 货币市场工具	4	97	94
3．其他投资	−2 528	19 694	22 222
3.1 资产	−3 030	995	4 025
3.1.1 贸易信贷	−688	282	970
长期	−14	6	19
短期	−674	276	950
3.1.2 贷款	−738	177	915
长期	−455	0	455
短期	−282	177	459
3.1.3 货币和存款	−1 597	514	2 111
3.1.4 其他资产	−8	22	29
长期	0	0	0

　　① 我国国际收支平衡表按国际货币基金组织《国际收支手册》第五版规定的各项原则编制，采用复式记账原则记录所有发生在我国居民（不包括港、澳、台地区）与非居民之间的经济交易。本表计数采用四舍五入原则。

续表

项　目	差　额	贷　方	借　方
短期	−8	22	29
3.2 负债	502	18 699	18 197
3.2.1 贸易信贷	−21	154	174
长期	0	3	3
短期	−20	151	171
3.2.2 贷款	−343	17 464	17 807
长期	−57	511	569
短期	−286	16 953	17 239
3.2.3 货币和存款	814	994	180
3.2.4 其他负债	52	87	35
长期	58	64	6
短期	−6	23	29
三、储备资产	**-1 178**	**312**	**1 490**
3.1 货币黄金	0	0	0
3.2 特别提款权	1	1	1
3.3 在基金组织的储备头寸	10	13	4
3.4 外汇	−1 188	298	1 486
3.5 其他债权	0	0	0
四、净误差与遗漏	**-1 401**	**0**	**1 401**

数据来源：国家外汇管理局。

专栏1

净误差与遗漏负值≠资本外逃规模

各国国际收支平衡表中都设有"净误差与遗漏"项目。根据国际标准，国际收支平衡表采用复式计账原则编制，为使平衡表在借贷两个方向上始终能够保持平衡，平衡表中设置了"净误差与遗漏"项。我国的国际收支平衡表编制以国际收支统计申报数据为基础，综合利用海关、人民银行、旅游局等其他相关数据。来自于多个部门和不同统计系统的数据，与国际收支统计在概念、口径、记录原则上不尽相同，同时，在各个部门的数据中，某些交易也难以全面记录，因此将这些数据汇总在国际收支平衡表中就可能会形成误差与遗漏。

我国误差与遗漏规模一直在合理范围内。根据国际惯例，平衡表中净误差与遗漏占同期货物进出口额的比重一般不宜超过正负5%。随着国际收支交易规模扩大，净误差与遗漏绝对数也会相应增加，高频数据比低频数据误差会更大。2008-2013年，我国平衡表中的该比例每年基本在2%左右；2014年第三、第四季度较高分别为5.6%和5.9%，但全年合计只有3.3%（见

图 C1-1

1994—2014 年我国误差与遗漏规模及占比情况

净误差与遗漏规模（左轴）　　　误差与遗漏占比（右轴）

数据来源：国家外汇管理局。

图 C1-1）。发达国家的平衡表中同样也有"净误差与遗漏"。以美国为例，其公布的 2014 年第二季度平衡表中，经常项目逆差 1 035 亿美元，资本项目顺差 103 亿美元，储备资产增加 8 亿美元，其误差与遗漏为正 940 亿美元，与同期货物进出口额之比为 9%；2012 年第一季度，其净误差与遗漏占比更是高达 15%。

净误差与遗漏负值不等于资本外逃规模。首先，净误差与遗漏方向与跨境资本流动没有必然关系。2009-2013 年，我国年度国际收支平衡表中净误差与遗漏均为负，但除 2012 年外，其他各年份我国面临的都是资本流入和人民币升值的压力。从国际上看，日本在 2007-2012 年、德国在 2003-2009 年均连续六七年呈现误差与遗漏为正，而其间欧元和日元有升有贬，宏观经济状况波动也很大（见图 C1-2）。其次，造成净误差与遗漏为负的原因也非常复杂，既有可能是低估了资本外流，也有可能是高估了经常项目顺差。国内外贸"奖出限入"、外资"宽进严出"的激励机制，本身也孕育了滋生这种现象的土壤。近年来，外汇局在检查中发现，有些企业出口不收汇或少收汇，存在高报出口骗取政府奖励或将收入违规留存境外的情况。最后，与日益健全的对外债务统计相比，我国对外债权统计较为薄弱，因此，即使是没有申报的资本流出也不一定是违规的，也可能是因制度原因而未被真实地记录。

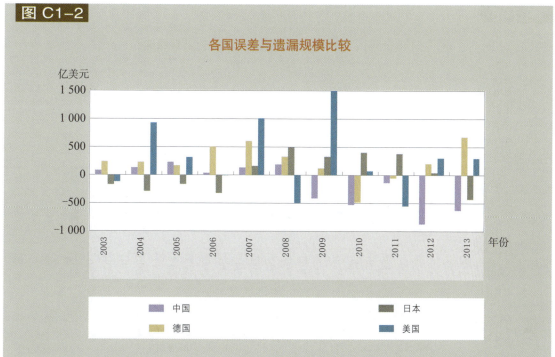

图 C1-2

各国误差与遗漏规模比较

数据来源：国际货币基金组织。

　　进一步提高国际收支统计质量。面对国际收支统计工作中层出不穷的新情况、新问题，外汇局正通过不断地改进统计制度和方法，尽可能地降低净误差与遗漏的规模。例如，近期实施的对外金融资产负债及交易统计制度，就既有负债又有资产的统计，同时区分了对外资产的交易变化和货币折算等非交易变化，这有助于减少非交易因素对统计质量的影响；该制度中新增加的银行卡境外刷卡消费统计，也可用于改进我国的旅游支出统计等。再如，除继续依靠基于企业调查制度，逐笔交易数据采集外，还将研究运用抽样调查和估算的方法，以更低的成本、更可靠的方式，确保国际收支统计的全面性和准确性。

（三）国际收支运行评价

　　促进国际收支平衡取得新进展。 2014 年，我国经常项目顺差与 GDP 之比为 2.1%，较上年增加 0.5 个百分点，仍处于国际公认的合理水平之内（见图 1-8）；国际收支口径的储备资产增加 1 178 亿美元，相当于 GDP 的 1.1%，较上年回落 3.4 个百分点。

　　跨境资本流动的波动性加强。 虽然全年我国国际收支呈现经常项目与资本项目

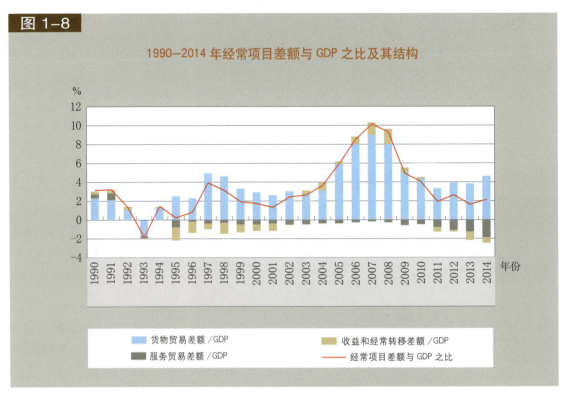

图 1-8

1990-2014 年经常项目差额与 GDP 之比及其结构

数据来源：国家外汇管理局、国家统计局。

图 1-9

2011-2014 年境内新增外汇存贷款与贷存比

数据来源：中国人民银行。

"双顺差"，但分季度看，跨境资本流动的顺逆差转换加快。其中，第一季度延续了2013年底的净流入态势，资本和金融项目顺差940亿美元。第二季度以来，受人民币汇率双向波动明显增强、国内外经济金融环境变化等因素影响，跨境资本呈现偏流出压力，推动我国国际收支呈现"经常项目顺差、资本和金融项目逆差"。第二至第四季度，在货物贸易顺差扩大、经常项目盈余增加的情况下，资本和金融项目分别转为逆差162亿美元、90亿美元和305亿美元。

藏汇于民和债务偿还是外汇分流的主要方式。在人民币汇率趋于均衡合理水平且双向波动明显增强的情况下，境内企业和个人调整优化了资产负债表。2014年，新增境内外汇存款1 084亿美元，新增外汇贷款204亿美元（见图1–9）。外汇存贷差部分被银行在境外运用，是推动其他投资资产项下我国对外贷款和资金存放境外等大幅增长的重要原因，显示了外汇资产由国家集中持有转向市场主体分散持有，但其控制权仍为境内主体。同期，其他投资负债项下（即境外对我国的贷款、贸易信贷和资金存放等）净流入502亿美元，但全年增幅较上年下降77%，这反映了境内企业加速偿还前期借了大量美元债务的影响。2014年，进口跨境融资余额减少449亿美元，上年为增加1 027亿美元（见图1–10）。

当前国际收支变化是预期的可承受的调整。随着人民币汇率形成机制市场化改革推进，央行逐步退出常态式外汇市场干预，必然是贸易顺差越大、资本流出越多。

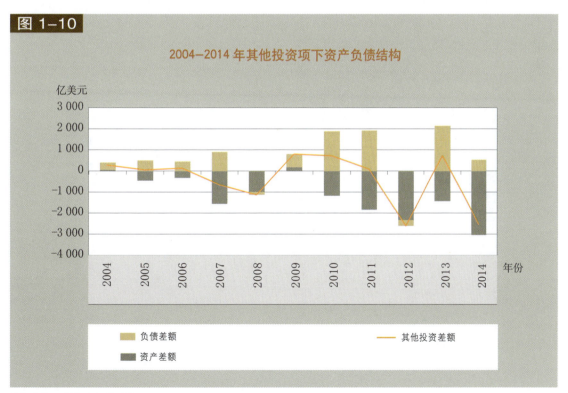

图 1–10

2004—2014年其他投资项下资产负债结构

数据来源：国家外汇管理局。

而且，"藏汇于民"体现了市场主体持汇意愿增强，符合调控目标和改革方向，有利于外汇供求平衡、改善宏观调控。"债务去杠杆化"也有利于企业部门减少货币错配，更好地应对资本流动冲击。更为重要的是，2014年第二季度以来资本流出压力加大并未改变全年国际收支"双顺差"的格局，外汇储备资产继续增加，且增幅较上次流出压力较大的2012年扩大20%。

二、国际收支主要
项目分析

（一）货物贸易

据海关统计，2014年我国货物贸易呈现以下特点。

进出口增速明显下滑。 2014年，我国进出口总额同比增长3.4%，低于上年7.6%的增幅，其中，出口和进口分别增长6.1%和0.4%。内需疲软、大宗商品价格下跌和上年套利贸易垫高基数是2014年进出口增速放缓的重要因素。据商务部测算[①]，剔除2013年套利贸易垫高基数因素后，2014年全国进出口同比实际增长6.1%，其中出口和进口实际增长8.7%和3.3%。同时，外贸依存度（进出口总额/GDP）进一步降至42%，较上年回落3个百分点，较2006年历史高点回落23个百分点（见图2-1），显示我国经济增长的内生性进一步增强。

进出口顺差继续扩大。 2014年，我国进出口顺差3825亿美元，同比扩大47.3%。进口价格回落是造成进出口顺差扩大的重要因素。在国内工业品和国际大宗商品价格普遍下跌的情况下，全年进口商品价格指数下降3.3%。其中，原油进口量同比增9.5%，进口额仅增3.9%；铁矿砂进口量增13.8%，进口额下降11.8%；煤及褐煤进口量下降10.9%，进口额下降23.5%。国内需求增速放缓、进口大宗商品贸易融资退潮等因素，也对进口增长产生影响。2014年，我国固定资产投资同比名义增长15.7%，

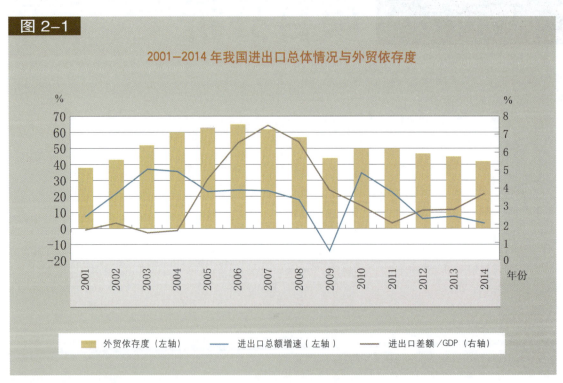

图 2-1

2001—2014年我国进出口总体情况与外贸依存度

图例：外贸依存度（左轴）　进出口总额增速（左轴）　进出口差额/GDP（右轴）

数据来源：海关总署、国家统计局。

[①] 详见商务部2015年1月21日例行新闻发布会，网址 http://www.mofcom.gov.cn/xwfbh/20150121.shtml。

增速较上年回落 3.9 个百分点。以铜为例，其贸易融资率在 2013 年第一季度为 89%，但 2014 年下半年以来明显下降，第三季度降至 2%，第四季度转为负值。进出口顺差扩大不是我国刻意追求的目标，但顺差扩大客观上增强了我国抵御资本流动冲击的能力，2014 年进出口顺差与同期 GDP 之比为 3.7%，较前两年略有提升（见图 2-1）。

贸易结构调整进一步优化。 从贸易方式上看，一般贸易在贸易总额中的占比为 53.8%，较上年提高 1 个百分点，比重连续两年提高。加工贸易占比进一步回落至 32.8%，远低于 2005 年近 50% 的比重（见图 2-2）。从外贸主体看，民营企业占外贸企业总数的比重超过 70%，较上年提高 1.6 个百分点，进出口量占贸易总额的 36.5%，较上年提高 0.6 个百分点，对整体进出口增量贡献 55.9%，成为外贸增长主力军（见图 2-3）。

贸易伙伴多元化趋势更加明显。 与发展中国家进出口比重较上年提高 0.4 个百分点，其中对东盟、印度、俄罗斯、非洲、中东欧国家等进出口增速均高于整体增速。对发达国家市场保持稳定增长，全年对欧盟和美国进出口分别增长 9.9% 和 6.6%。尽管 2014 年我国进出口增速下滑，但预计将高于全球平均增速，第一货物贸易大国地位进一步巩固。2014 年我国出口商品在美国、欧盟和日本等主要贸易伙伴的市场份额微幅上升，分别较上年上升 0.5 个、1.4 个和 0.6 个百分点，出口市场份额连续两年回升。

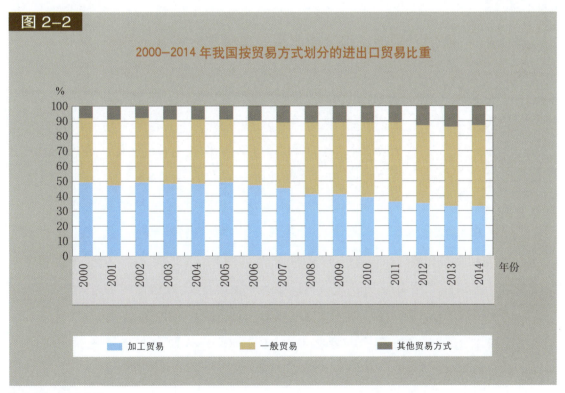

图 2-2

2000—2014 年我国按贸易方式划分的进出口贸易比重

加工贸易　　　一般贸易　　　其他贸易方式

数据来源：海关总署。

图 2-3

2000—2014 年我国按外贸主体划分的进出口贸易比重

数据来源：海关总署。

专栏 2

"海淘"带动我国跨境电子商务外汇收支快速增长

　　跨境电子商务是我国对外贸易的新增长点，"海淘"在我国日渐盛行。顺应形势发展，外汇局于 2013 年推出了支付机构跨境电子商务外汇支付业务试点，便利跨境电子商务的外汇收付。2014 年，全国共有 22 家支付机构参与试点，通过试点业务办理的跨境电子商务外汇收支快速增长。

　　个人跨境网购热情高涨。通过试点业务，2014 年支付机构累计办理跨境电子商务外汇收支 17 亿美元。我国居民个人跨境网购活跃，试点业务中仅个人跨境网购支出（含个人服务贸易支出）超过 15 亿美元，占总收支额的 88.5%。因梅西百货等境外大型零售网站与我国支付机构的对接，加入"海淘"的个人不断增多，跨境网购支出金额逐月增长；特别在 11 月、12 月受西方国家节日打折促销及国内网络购物活动影响，个人跨境网购支出连续两个月突破 2 亿美元。

图 C2-1

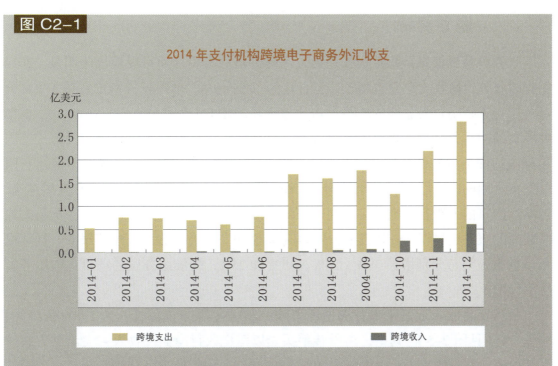

2014 年支付机构跨境电子商务外汇收支

数据来源：国家外汇管理局。

　　服务贸易在跨境电子商务中的优势逐渐显现。为保证交易真实性，试点业务范围包括货物贸易及具有真实交易背景的部分服务贸易。2014 年上半年货物贸易收支一直高于服务贸易收支，第三季度服务贸易收支后来居上，至第四季度，因传统购物旺季到来，"海淘"业务激增，货物贸易收支再次超过服务贸易收支，全年货物贸易收支占比为 56.3%。总体来看，尽管货物贸易收支比重较大，但服务贸易在电子商务交易中的优势正逐渐显现，第四季度服务贸易交易额占比较第一季度提高 6 个百分点。

　　试点业务发展不均衡。试点业务办理主要集中在少数支付机构，个别机构对服务贸易支付服务优势明显，多数支付机构业务仍有待拓展。同时，试点业务中进口业务拓展明显优于出口，跨境电子商务外汇支出在试点业务中占绝对多数。此外，支付机构有待开拓出口市场，将海外消费者引进中国。

　　为进一步支持跨境电子商务发展，国家外汇管理局于 2015 年 1 月发布《关于开展支付机构跨境外汇支付业务试点的通知》，允许全国范围内符合条件的支付机构参与试点业务，并对试点业务的业务范围及单笔限额进一步放宽。

（二）服务贸易

服务贸易规模保持稳定增长趋势，高附加值服务贸易项目规模增速明显。2014
年我国服务贸易收支总额达到 5 738 亿美元，增长 7%，增速较货物贸易高 3 个百分
点，相当于货物贸易总额的 14%，占比较上年略增 0.4 个百分点（见图 2-4）。根据
世界贸易组织每年发布的《全球贸易报告》，2004 年我国服务贸易额与美国、德国
和英国的服务贸易额比例分别为 22%、40% 和 42%，到 2013 年，我国与上述三国
服务贸易额的比例已分别上升到 49%、88% 和 114%，表明我国服务贸易发展迅速，
与发达国家的差距在不断缩小。在国家优化服务贸易结构的政策导向下，贸易附加
值较高的服务项目得到较快发展，2014 年金融服务、通讯服务、建筑服务、计算机
和信息服务贸易分别增长 38%、24%、38% 和 25%，传统服务贸易项目运输服务贸
易额仅增长 2%。

服务贸易收入近五年来首次出现下降。2014 年服务贸易收入为 1 909 亿美元，
减少 7%（见图 2-5）。其中，离岸转手买卖以跨境收付净额（收入 – 支出）方式计
入其他商业服务的贷方，由上年的净流入 223 亿美元转为 2014 年净流出 95 亿美元。
主要是相关企业延期支付的境外融资减少而到期偿付增多，导致其他商业服务收入
金额全年仅为 14 亿美元，减少 327 亿美元，降幅达 96%。

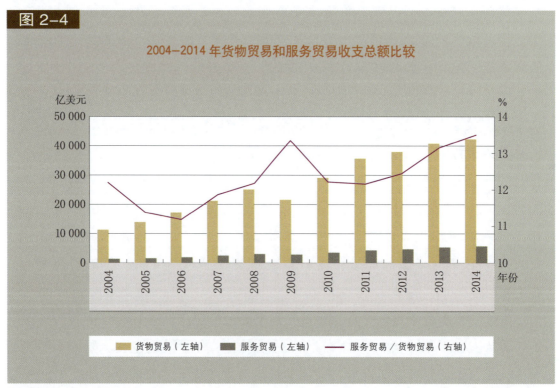

图 2-4

2004－2014 年货物贸易和服务贸易收支总额比较

数据来源：国家外汇管理局。

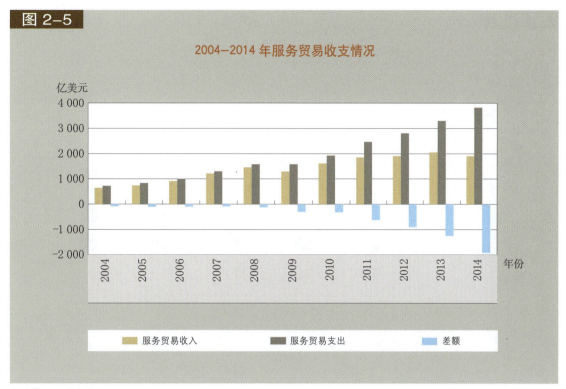

图 2-5

2004—2014 年服务贸易收支情况

亿美元

■ 服务贸易收入　　■ 服务贸易支出　　■ 差额

数据来源：国家外汇管理局。

服务贸易支出快速增长，旅游支出占比持续上升。2014 年服务贸易支出 3 829 亿美元（见图 2-5），增长 16%。其中，旅游支出占服务贸易支出的 43%，增加 4 个百分点，是服务贸易支出占比最大项目；运输支出为第二大项目，但近五年占比不断减少，2014 年占比 25%，减少 4 个百分点；其他项目支出占比变动较平稳。

服务贸易逆差继续扩大，旅游逆差快速增长是主因。2014 年服务贸易逆差 1 920 亿美元，增长 54%，其中在服务贸易额中占比近四成的旅游项目是服务贸易整体逆差扩大的主要来源（见图 2-6）。由于居民可支配收入提高，出境旅游及留学人数和人均花费均较快增加。2014 年旅游项目支出 1 649 亿美元，增长 28%；收入 569 亿美元，增长 10%；逆差 1 079 亿美元，增长 40%，对当期服务贸易逆差的贡献度为 56%。

逆差国家和地区集中度有所降低，顺差仍高度集中在香港地区。2014 年，我国对前十大服务贸易伙伴国（地区）的服务贸易总体呈现逆差，逆差规模达 245 亿美元，较上年减少 18%；对前十大逆差国家和地区的服务贸易逆差合计 751 亿美元，占当年服务贸易逆差 40%，下降 20 个百分点。2014 年，我国逆差额较大的国家（地区）包括美国、新加坡、韩国和澳大利亚，分别逆差 171 亿美元、106 亿美元、97 亿美元和 94 亿美元；我国对香港地区服务贸易顺差 433 亿美元，增长 36%，在顺差国家和地区中占比 93%（见图 2-7）。

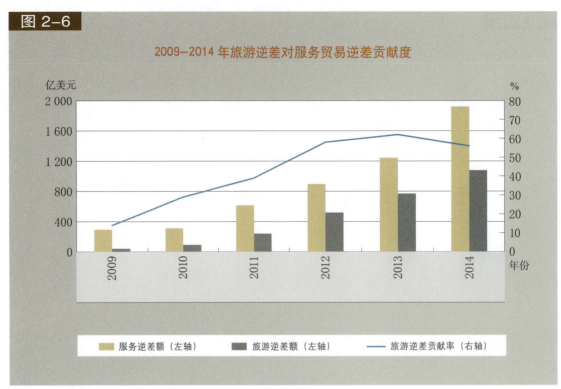

图 2-6

2009-2014 年旅游逆差对服务贸易逆差贡献度

服务逆差额（左轴）　　旅游逆差额（左轴）　　旅游逆差贡献率（右轴）

数据来源：国家外汇管理局。

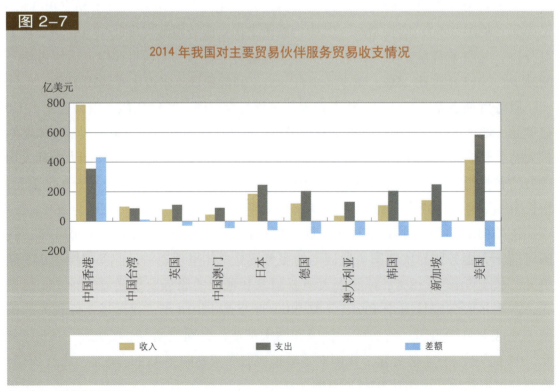

图 2-7

2014 年我国对主要贸易伙伴服务贸易收支情况

收入　　支出　　差额

数据来源：国家外汇管理局。

专栏3

当前服务贸易收支状况基本正常

服务贸易逆差由来已久，反映了我国服务业相对滞后的结构性问题。2014年，我国服务贸易逆差增长675亿美元，达到1 920亿美元，引起社会各界广泛关注。实际上，自1995年开始，我国服务贸易就已连年逆差，近年来逆差规模不断扩大，2011年逆差增长曾达到98%。长期逆差反映了我国的服务贸易国际竞争力相对较低，缺乏比较优势。我国服务贸易发展相对滞后于货物贸易，服务贸易与货物贸易的比例长期偏低，我国二者比例在1∶7左右，发达国家平均水平在1∶3。特别在高附加值服务方面，我国的差距更为明显。

近几年服务贸易逆差扩大，体现了我国居民收入水平提高所带来的消费升级。在我国居民收入持续增长和人民币汇率不断走强的带动下，近几年，居民境外实际购买力大幅提高，出境旅游、留学、海外网上购物等成本普遍下降，需求日益旺盛。近年来，我国居民出境人次快速增长，2014年首次突

图 C3-1

2001-2014年入境游客与内地居民出境人次

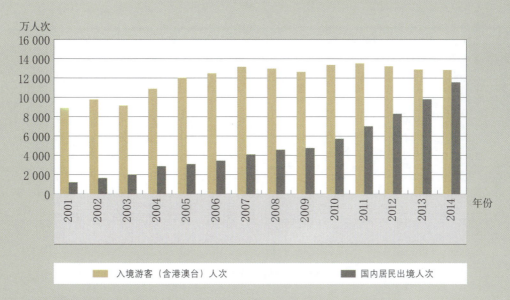

数据来源：国家旅游局。

破上亿人次，增长 18%（见图 C3-1）。出境人数和花费的增长带动旅游支出不断扩大。据联合国世界旅游组织统计，自 2012 年起中国跃升为世界第一大国际旅游消费国，2013 年境外消费额达 1 290 亿美元，在上年增长 40% 的基础上又增长了 26%，比美国还多出 420 亿美元。因此，国内居民切实享受了改革开放带来的好处。

各项便利化措施推动我国服务贸易支出增长，特别是出境旅游支出增长。随着我国对外开放步伐加快和国力增强，我国居民境外旅游目的地不断增加，各国和地区纷纷推出免签、落地签、自由行等吸引中国游客的优惠政策。外汇管理方面也加大改革力度，提高个人年度购汇额度，大幅简化购付汇手续，支持通过银行卡和第三方支付机构进行境外消费，保证持卡人偿还境外消费的用汇需求等。在推动贸易便利化的同时，外汇局也采取了相应措施应对跨境资金流动风险。如单笔超过 5 万美元的收付汇仍需审核交易单证，必要时进行现场核查和检查等。

服务贸易逆差有利于实现国际收支平衡的宏观调控目标。2014 年，国际收支口径的货物贸易顺差增长 32%，被服务贸易逆差的扩大部分抵消，货物

图 C3-2

1994-2014 年货物和服务贸易差额及其与 GDP 之比

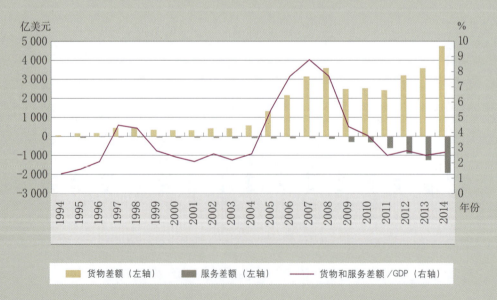

数据来源：国家外汇管理局、国家统计局。

和服务贸易合计顺差 2 840 亿美元，增幅收敛至 21%，货物和服务贸易顺差占国内生产总值的比重为 2.7%，经常项目顺差仍处于健康合理的水平上（见图 C3-2）。

（三）直接投资

直接投资净流入略有下降。2014 年，我国国际收支口径的直接投资流入 4 352 亿美元，流出 2 266 亿美元，同比分别增长 14% 和 39%。净流入 2 087 亿美元，下降 4%。同年，经常项目和直接投资差额之和（即基础性国际收支差额）共计 4 284 亿美元，同比增长 17%，占国内生产总值的 4.1%，占比较上年上升 0.3 个百分点，进一步增强了我国抵御资本流动冲击的能力（见图 2-8）。

外国来华直接投资（FDI）净流入总体平稳。2014 年，FDI 净流入 2 891 亿美元，同比下降 1%（见图 2-9）。FDI 流入 3 797 亿美元，增长 10%。其中，股本投资流入 1 456 亿美元，收益再投资流入 1 292 亿美元，其他资本（主要含外商投资企业与境外关联企业间贷款及往来款等）流入 1 049 亿美元，同比分别增长 4%、下降 10% 和增长 72%。FDI 流出 906 亿美元，增长 70%，其中，与境外关联方贷款及往来款流出 734 亿美元，增长 107%。在我国宏观经济基本面呈现结构调整阵痛期、增

图 2-8

2000–2014 年基础性国际收支差额与 GDP 之比

数据来源：国家外汇管理局、国家统计局。

图 2-9

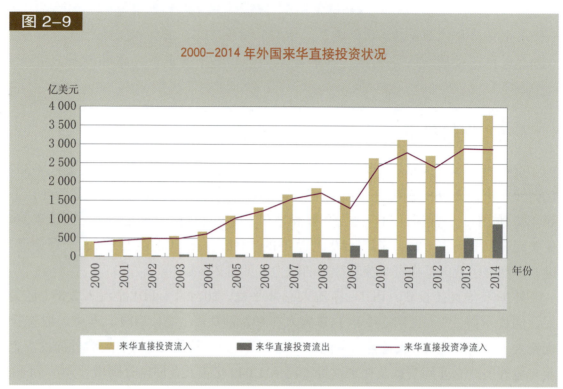

2000—2014 年外国来华直接投资状况

数据来源：国家外汇管理局。

图 2-10

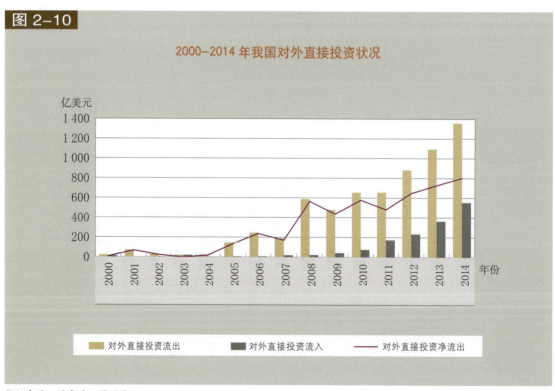

2000—2014 年我国对外直接投资状况

数据来源：国家外汇管理局。

图 2-11

2014 年我国非金融部门对外直接投资流出分布
（按国内行业、投资目的地划分）

数据来源：国家外汇管理局。

速换挡期和前期政策消化期"三期"叠加特点的情况下，外资仍保持长期投资中国的信心。同时，境内外融资环境和成本差异对境内外关联企业间融资行为产生一定影响（参见《2014 年中国跨境资金流动监测报告》第二部分"直接投资"项目的分析）。

我国对外直接投资（ODI）继续快速增长。2014 年，我国 ODI 流出 1 359 亿美元，回流 555 亿美元，净流出 804 亿美元，同比分别增长 24%、53% 和 10%（见图 2-10）。分部门看，金融部门 ODI 净流出 116 亿美元，同比下降 26%，主要是由于银行部门境外股本投资 33 亿美元，下降 46%；非金融部门 ODI 净流出 689 亿美元，增长 20%，反映出中国境内企业"走出去"步伐总体上仍在加快，且国内"走出去"行业和主要投资目的地较为集中（见图 2-11）。国内企业大型海外并购进展明显。2014 年，中国企业在能源矿产、制造业和农业等多个投资领域并购活跃，如五矿资源等企业联营体收购秘鲁拉斯邦巴斯铜矿，国家电网公司收购意大利存贷款能源网公司股权，联想集团收购美国摩托罗拉公司移动手机业务，东风汽车有限公司收购法国标致雪铁龙集团股权，等等。其中，中粮集团并购新加坡来宝农业公司和荷兰尼德拉公司，成为迄今为止农业领域最大的两个对外投资项目。

（四）证券投资

证券投资延续顺差格局。2014 年，我国证券投资项下净流入 824 亿美元，较上年增长 56%（见图 2-12）。自 2011 年美欧主权债务危机之后，连续三年出现由于境外对我国证券投资增长而形成的证券投资净流入。与一般新兴市场跨境证券投资的大进大出不同，境外不断加大对中国的证券投资，体现了在中国经济稳步增长的背景下，资本市场逐步完善且对外开放不断扩大的吸引力。

注：我国对外证券投资正值表示净回流，负值表示净流出；境外对我国证券投资正值表示净流入，负值表示净流出。
数据来源：国家外汇管理局。

    我国对外证券投资规模小但增长较快。2014 年，我国对外证券投资净流出 108 亿美元，较上年增长 1 倍。随着海外资本市场尤其是美国债市持续升温，境内主体海外投资热情较高。从投资种类看，对外股本投资与债券投资规模相当但后者净流出较多，对外债券投资呈现净流出 94 亿美元，对外股本投资净流出 14 亿美元。这种重债市的投资方式显示境内主体投资风险偏好下降，避险情绪上升。从投资主体看，一是银行部门增加对外债券投资，全年银行部门对外债券投资净流出 32 亿美元，较上年增长 3.8 倍；二是合格境内机构投资者（QDII）净汇出资金 96 亿美元，较上年增长 1.1 倍，创 2008 年国际金融危机以来的新高。

    境外对我国证券投资增长较快。2014 年，境外对我国证券投资净流入 932 亿美元，较上年增长 60%。其中，股本证券投资净流入 519 亿美元，债务证券投资净流入 413 亿美元，较上年分别增长 59% 和 61%。从投资渠道看，一是合格境外机构投资者（QFII）和人民币合格境外机构投资者（RQFII）境内投资快速增长，2014 年两者合计净流入 253 亿美元，较上年增长 51%，主要是因为 QFII 和 RQFII 投资额度增加，带动增长；二是其他境外机构运用人民币投资境内银行间债券市场继续增加，2014 年净流入 329 亿美元；三是境内机构 H 股筹资 342 亿美元，较上年快速增长 98%，这主要是大型企业和金融机构在港发行股票所致。

（五）其他投资

其他投资由上年的净流入转为净流出。其他投资项下资本流动是影响我国国际收支状况的重要因素。2014 年，该项资金流入和流出分别占资本和金融项下流入和流出的 77% 和 88%。由于国际和国内不确定因素增多，我国其他投资项下顺逆差转化频繁，波动性、顺周期性明显。2014 年，我国其他投资项下净流出 2 528 亿美元，上年为净流入 722 亿美元。其中，贷款、货币和存款及贸易信贷分别净流出 1 081 亿美元、783 亿美元和 708 亿美元，其他项下净流入 44 亿美元（见图 2-13）。

其他投资项下对外资本输出大幅增长。2014 年，我国其他投资项下对外资本输出净增加 3 030 亿美元，较上年增长 1.1 倍，主要反映了银行部门更多将资金运用于境外。其中，我国在境外的货币和存款增加 1 597 亿美元，而上年仅增加 74 亿美元，增长 20 倍；对境外贷款增加 738 亿美元，较上年增长 1.3 倍；对外提供的贸易信贷增加 688 亿美元，较上年增长 14%。其他投资项下对外资本输出的增长，反映了境内主体对境内外汇率、利率及市场的预期变化，扩大了资金的境外运用。

其他投资项下对外负债继续增加但增幅下降。2014 年，境外对我国其他投资项下资金净流入（即我国对外负债净增加）502 亿美元，较上年下降 77%。一是我国吸收的货币和存款类资金增加 814 亿美元，较上年增长 7%，主要是非居民人民币存

图 2-13

2000—2014 年其他投资各组成部分净额

数据来源：国家外汇管理局。

款增加 647 亿美元；二是获得的境外贷款由上年增加 934 亿美元转为减少 343 亿美元，主要是由于银行为规避信用证、海外代付等贸易融资工具风险，从而大幅减少了该类对外负债。

专栏 4

宏观审慎管理在银行外汇收支管理中的实践

2008 年国际金融危机爆发后，各国际组织和监管机构开始意识到，单独依靠微观审慎管理防范和应对金融体系顺周期性与跨部门风险不能奏效，宏观审慎管理日益受到国际关注和重视。同样，在国内外汇管理践行"五个转变"的过程中，如何淡化对企业和个人的微观管理，加强对银行外汇收支整体的审慎监管，逐步建立逆周期调节机制，减轻乃至熨平跨境资金流动大幅波动对经济可能产生的冲击，对于外汇管理部门十分重要。

一、银行外汇收支宏观审慎管理的两次实践与运用

2010 年末至 2011 年初出台收付实现制头寸管理措施。2010 年第四季度，由于人民币升值预期明显上升，银行对客户远期签约净结汇快速增长。为对冲自身外汇风险敞口，银行在即期市场提前卖出外汇头寸（造成收付实现制头寸下降），引起央行净购汇大幅增加。为此，国家外汇管理局（以下简称外汇局）分别于 2010 年 11 月和 2011 年 3 月下发了通知，对银行按照收付实现制原则计算的头寸余额实行下限管理，限制银行远期结售汇敞口通过即期市场平盘，促使银行及时调整远期结售汇报价，并由此对客户远期结售汇规模形成约束，应对跨境资金异常的流入。政策出台后，银行对客户未到期远期差额不再上升，缓解了央行购汇压力，同时由于银行增持了外汇头寸规模，抵御风险能力得到提升，平滑了 2011 年底外汇市场震荡带来的外汇增持压力（见图 C4-1）。2012 年 4 月，在外汇供求趋于平衡，跨境资金异常流入情况缓解后，外汇局及时取消了这一临时性限制措施。

2013 年 5 月出台结售汇综合头寸下限管理措施。2012 年底以来，人民币升值预期有所恢复，我国企业和个人等非银行部门结售汇顺差从低位大幅回升，2013 年反弹速度进一步加快，第一季度顺差达 1 693 亿美元，其中一个重要原因是企业利用银行的国内外汇贷款替代购汇。为此，外汇局调整对

2010−2012 年未到期远期差额和收付实现制头寸比较情况

数据来源：国家外汇管理局。

银行结售汇综合头寸的管理，将银行结售汇综合头寸限额与外汇存、贷款规模挂钩，对于银行外汇贷存比（境内外汇贷款余额／外汇存款余额）超过参考贷存比的银行，要求其在规定的时限内将综合头寸调整至下限以上。政策出台后，银行一方面增持结售汇综合头寸；另一方面控制并压缩国内外汇贷款规模，国内外汇贷款规模逐月下降，国内外汇贷存比得到了控制（见图C4-2）。2014 年 12 月，外汇局适应外汇供求形势的变化，及时取消了这一临时性限制措施。

二、银行外汇收支宏观审慎管理的展望

首先，银行外汇收支规模快速增长，为银行境内外资金摆布和非银行部门财务运作提供了丰富的资金来源，具有顺周期特点。银行通过自身对外资产负债摆布、境内外融资、人民币外汇衍生交易，与人民币升值预期形成共振，顺周期推动了企业境内外财务运作，加大了外汇市场波动和外汇储备增长压力。

其次，银行外汇收支宏观审慎管理应侧重于跨境收支宏观审慎的逆周期调节，有效防范跨境资金异常流动，促进国际收支基本平衡。为实现这一目标，

图 C4-2

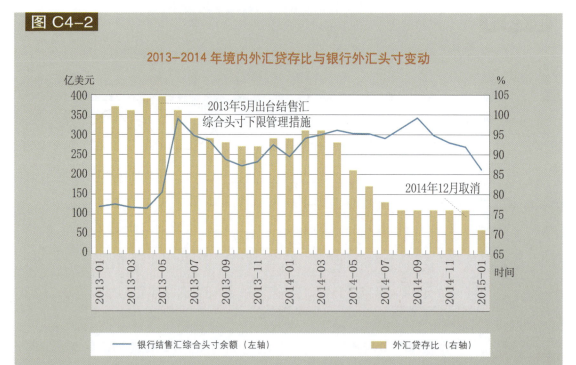

2013-2014年境内外汇贷存比与银行外汇头寸变动

注：剔除了政策性银行。
数据来源：中国人民银行、国家外汇管理局。

应从宏观、中观、微观三个层面加强监测，构建银行外汇收支异常波动监测体系；在政策选择层面，要区分常规管理政策、"临时性冲击"政策、"实质性冲击"政策三个层面。对于"临时性冲击"，应以市场化手段调控；对于"实质性冲击"，应采取资本流动管理措施并辅之以宏观审慎措施保障金融稳定。

最后，实施银行外汇收支宏观审慎管理，应加强调控对象的分析和政策工具的具体设计。从调控角度看，银行的外汇负债、外汇资产和表外融资业务均是可调控的对象。在政策工具选择上，一是要深入研究银行结售汇综合头寸的市场化调节作用；二是完善和改进其他现有管理手段，包括银行短期外债指标管理、银行执行外汇管理规定考核运用；三是借鉴国际经验，充实政策工具储备。

三、国际投资
头寸状况

对外金融净资产有所缩减。2014 年末，我国对外金融资产 [①]64 087 亿美元，对外负债 46 323 亿美元，分别较上年末增长 7% 和 16%，对外金融开放度（对外金融资产与负债之和 / 国内生产总值）为 107%，较上年上升 1.5 个百分点；对外净资产为 17 764 亿美元，较上年末减少 2 196 亿美元，与国内生产总值之比为 17%，较上年下降 3.9 个百分点（见图 3–1 和图 3–2）。对外净资产缩减 [②]，一是由于汇率和价格等非交易原因，以储备资产为主的对外金融资产出现较大的账面价值波动；二是部分机构向上修正其对外负债历史数据，导致年末对外负债增长。

对外金融资产变化体现"藏汇于民"。2014 年末，国际储备资产余额为 38 993 亿美元，继续占据对外金融资产首位，占资产总值的比重为 61%，占比较上年末减少 4.0 个百分点，为 2004 年以来的最低。民间部门正在加快"走出去"，因风险偏好较低，更青睐传统投资渠道，对外直接投资和存贷款等其他投资资产共计 22 469 亿美元，占资产总值的比重升全历年最高值（35%）；而对外证券投资资产 2 625 亿美元，占比 4%，较上年末略降 0.2 个百分点（见图 3–3）。

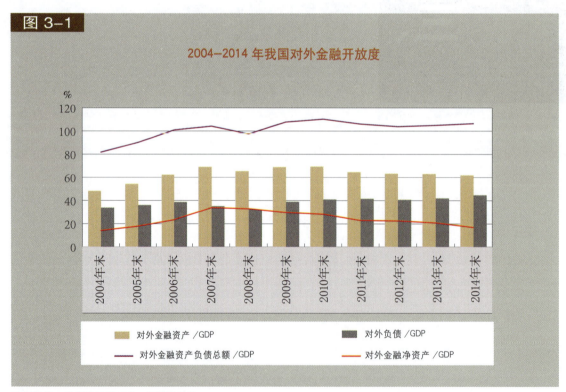

图 3–1

2004–2014 年我国对外金融开放度

- 对外金融资产 /GDP
- 对外负债 /GDP
- 对外金融资产负债总额 /GDP
- 对外金融净资产 /GDP

数据来源：国家外汇管理局、国家统计局。

---

① 对外金融资产和负债包括直接投资、证券投资及存贷款等其他投资。之所以对外直接投资属于金融资产范畴，是因为境内投资者持有的是境外被投资企业的股权，这与证券投资中的股权投资无本质区别，只是直接投资通常持股比例较高，意在影响或控制企业的生产经营活动。反之，外来直接投资则属于对外金融负债范畴，也是境外投资者对外商投资企业的权益。

② 对外净资产变动不等于国际收支平衡表经常项目差额，具体分析参见《2013 年中国国际收支报告》专栏 3。

图 3-2

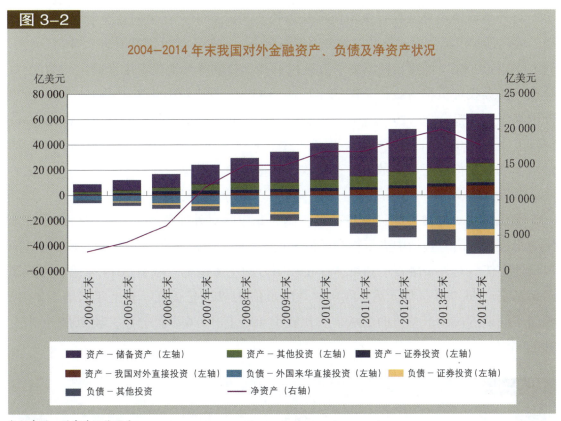

2004—2014 年末我国对外金融资产、负债及净资产状况

数据来源：国家外汇管理局。

图 3-3

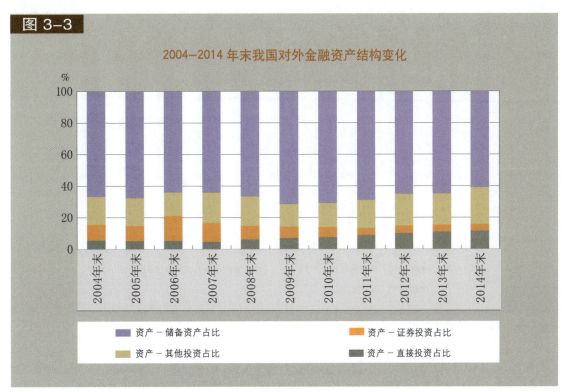

2004—2014 年末我国对外金融资产结构变化

数据来源：国家外汇管理局。

　　对外负债中对外证券投资负债增长较快。2014 年末，在境内企业赴境外上市升温、境内证券市场加大对外开放等多因素影响下，对外证券投资负债达 5 143 亿美元，较上年增长 33%，增速较外国来华直接投资和存贷款等其他投资增速高出约 20 个百分点。证券投资负债占负债总额的比重达到 11%，占比较上年末上升 1.4 个百分点。外国来华直接投资 26 779 亿美元 ①，增长 15%，继续位列对外负债首位，占比 58%，但较上年下降 0.6 个百分点。受境内外汇率、利率变化以及人民币国际化等影响，同时由于部分机构修正历史数据，存贷款等其他投资负债增长 13%，达到 14 402 亿美元，占负债总额的 31%，占比较上年下降 0.8 个百分点（见图 3-4）。

　　民间部门对外净负债进一步扩张。作为非成熟对外净债权人，我国对外净资产集中于公共部门（包括中央银行和政府部门），而银行和企业等民间部门则为对外净负债的主体，对外金融资产和负债存在较明显的主体错配。截至 2014 年末，剔除国际储备资产 38 993 亿美元后，我国对外净负债 21 229 亿美元，较上年末增长 13%，相当于同期国内生产总值的 20%，占比较上年末上升 0.6 个百分点，较 2008 年末上升 10 个百分点。

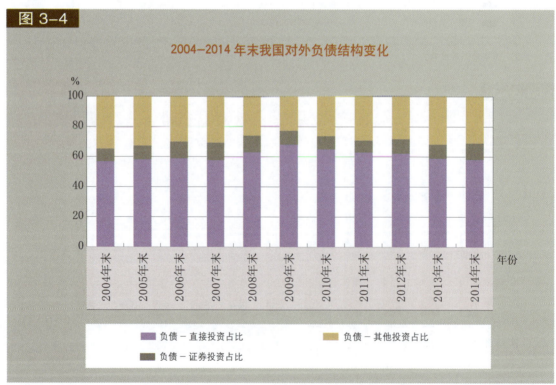

图 3-4

2004-2014 年末我国对外负债结构变化

数据来源：国家外汇管理局。

---

　　① 外国来华直接投资存量包括我国非金融部门和金融部门吸收来华直接投资存量，以及境内外母子公司间贷款和其他债务性往来，反映了价值重估因素影响。该口径与商务部统计的累计吸收外商直接投资不同，其数据是历年外商直接投资股本投资流量累加。

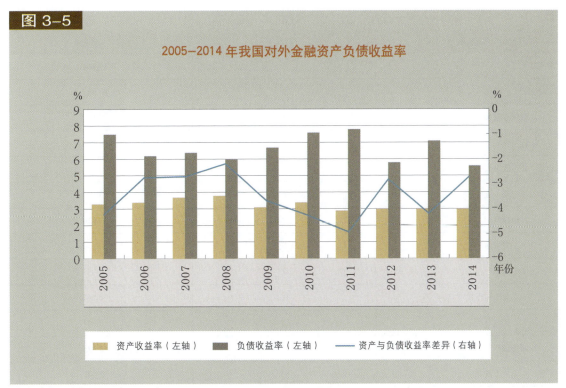

图 3-5

2005—2014 年我国对外金融资产负债收益率

资产收益率（左轴）　　负债收益率（左轴）　　资产与负债收益率差异（右轴）

注：1. 资产（或负债）收益率＝（年度投资收益收入（或支出））/［（上年末＋本年末对外金融资产（或负债）存量）/2］。
　　2. 资产负债收益率差异＝资产收益率－负债收益率。
数据来源：国家外汇管理局。

　　对外投资收益呈现结构性逆差。2014 年，我国国际收支平衡表中投资收益为逆差 599 亿美元，其中，我国对外投资收益收入 1 831 亿美元，对外负债收益支出 2 429 亿美元，二者收益率差异为 –2.7 个百分点，为 2009 年以来差异最小的一年（见图 3-5）。投资收益为负与我国对外金融资产负债的持有主体有关，使我国与市场化程度较高、以民间对外金融资产负债为主的经济体不可类比。实际上，我国对外投资收益与国际相比并不低，但因为近六成外来投资是外国来华直接投资，其回报较高，导致轧差后投资收益为负值（具体分析详见《2012 年中国国际收支报告》专栏 1）。不过，通过利用外国来华直接投资，我国不仅吸引了资金，还引进了外方先进技术和管理经验，创造了国内就业和税收，开拓了国际市场，其社会效应和经济收益远大于财务成本。同时，外方收益支出中有相当部分是再投资收益，这部分收益又投回了企业，并没有实际的资金流出，扣除这一块，我国投资收益仍为净收入。

表 3-1　2014 年中国国际投资头寸表[①]　　　　　　　　　　　　　　单位：亿美元

项目	行次	2014 年末
净头寸[②]	1	17 764
A. 资产	2	64 087
1. 对外直接投资	3	7 443
2. 证券投资	4	2 625
2.1 股本证券	5	1 613
2.2 债务证券	6	1 012
3. 其他投资	7	15 026
3.1 贸易信贷	8	4 677
3.2 贷款	9	3 747
3.3 货币和存款	10	5 541
3.4 其他资产	11	1 061
4. 储备资产	12	38 993
4.1 货币黄金	13	401
4.2 特别提款权	14	105
4.3 在基金组织中的储备头寸	15	57
4.4 外汇	16	38 430
B. 负债	17	46 323
1. 外国来华直接投资	18	26 779
2. 证券投资	19	5 143
2.1 股本证券	20	3 693
2.2 债务证券	21	1 449
3. 其他投资	22	14 402
3.1 贸易信贷	23	3 344
3.2 贷款	24	5 720
3.3 货币和存款	25	5 030
3.4 其他负债	26	308

数据来源：国家外汇管理局。

---

①　与国际收支平衡表一致，国际投资头寸表同样遵循居民统计原则，即无论本币或外币，只要发生在居民与非居民之间，均需要记录。

②　净头寸是指资产减负债，"+"表示净资产，"-"表示净负债。本表计算采用四舍五入原则。

四、外汇市场运行与人民币汇率

（一）人民币汇率走势

人民币对美元汇率小幅下跌。2014年末，人民币对美元汇率中间价为6.1190元/美元，较上年末下跌0.4%（见图4–1），银行间外汇市场（CNY）和境外市场（CNH）即期交易价累计分别下跌2.4%和2.6%，但在全球范围内仍属于较为稳定的货币（见图4–2）。

人民币对一篮子货币多边汇率升值。据国际清算银行（BIS）测算，2014年人民币名义有效汇率累计升值6.41%，扣除通货膨胀因素的实际有效汇率累计升值6.39%（见图4–3），在BIS监测的61种货币中升值幅度分别居第5位和第8位。2005年汇改以来，人民币名义和实际有效汇率累计分别升值40.5%和51.3%，在BIS监测的61种货币中升值幅度分别居第1位和第2位。

人民币汇率双向浮动弹性增强。从即期汇率（即CNY）看（见图4–4），2014年年初至2月中旬，银行间外汇市场即期交易价保持稳定，并整体贴近中间价浮动区间下限。2月下旬开始，交易价持续下跌并转入中间价贬值区间，3月17日扩大汇率浮动区间后波幅进一步扩大，至4月末累计贬值2.8%。5月以后，交易价止跌企稳并逐步回升，8月重新转入中间价升值区间，5~10月累计升值2.4%。11月、12月，交易价再度走弱并逐步偏向中间价浮动区间上限，两个月累计贬值1.5%。从

图4–1
2014年境内外人民币对美元即期汇率走势

数据来源：中国外汇交易中心、路透数据库。

图 4-2

全球主要发达和新兴市场货币对美元汇率变动

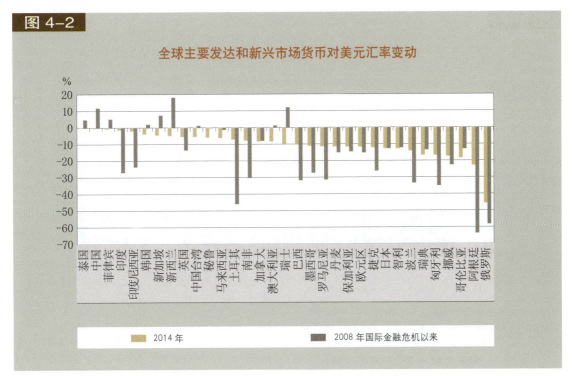

数据来源：中国外汇交易中心、彭博资讯。

图 4-3

1994 年 1 月至 2014 年 12 月人民币有效汇率走势

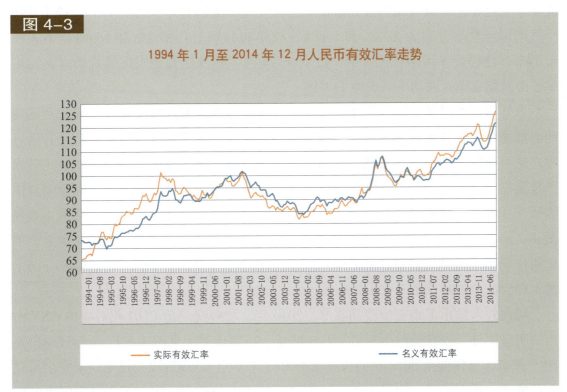

数据来源：国际清算银行。

图 4-4

2014 年银行间外汇市场人民币对美元即期交易价波动情况

最低价偏离中间价幅度（左轴）　　　　　最高价偏离中间价幅度（左轴）

最高价 − 最低价（基点，右轴）

数据来源：中国外汇交易中心。

波动率变化看，2014 年境内外期权市场隐含波动率明显上升（见图 4-5），12 月末 6 个月期限波动率分别为 2.78% 和 3.47%，较年初分别上升 87.2% 和 86.8%。但人民币汇率弹性仍处于国际较低水平，12 月末 24 种主要发达和新兴市场货币对美元汇率 6 个月期权隐含波动率平均为 11.94%。

本外币利差增加推动远期外汇市场美元升水幅度扩大。2014 年，汇率、利率变动的市场化内在联系机制进一步增强。年初，企业大量远期净结汇压低美元升水点数，此后随着人民币汇率下跌，远期结汇需求下降、购汇意愿上升，推动美元升水点数走高。同时，外汇存款增加使境内美元流动性趋向宽松，而人民币资金面总体偏紧，令本外币利差逐渐扩大，利率平价机制引导美元升水点数扩大（见图 4-6 和图 4-7）。2014 年末，境内银行间远期市场、境外可交割远期市场和境外无本金交割远期市场 1 年期美元分别升水 1 585 个、1 550 个和 2 295 个基点，较上年末分别上涨 1 135 个、1 090 个和 2 034 个基点。

境内外人民币汇率差价波动收窄。2014 年，境外交易价 CNH 相对境内 CNY 由年初明显偏强、较宽价差逐渐转为双向波动、窄幅价差（见图 4-8），全年日均价差 79 个基点，整体低于 2013 年的价差水平（83 个基点）。现阶段人民币尚未完全可兑换环境下，供求关系、交易主体、监管政策等因素的差异，决定了人民币汇率在境

图 4-5

2012 年以来人民币对美元汇率 6 个月期权隐含波动率

注：平价期权隐含波动率。
数据来源：彭博资讯。

图 4-6

2013 年以来境内外人民币对美元远期市场 1 年期美元升贴水点数

数据来源：中国外汇交易中心、路透数据库。

图 4-7

2013 年以来境内人民币与美元利差（6 个月期限）

利差 2- 利差 1　　　　利差 1 (人民币 shibor 境内美元拆借)
利差 2 （外汇掉期隐含）

数据来源：中国外汇交易中心、路透数据库。

图 4-8

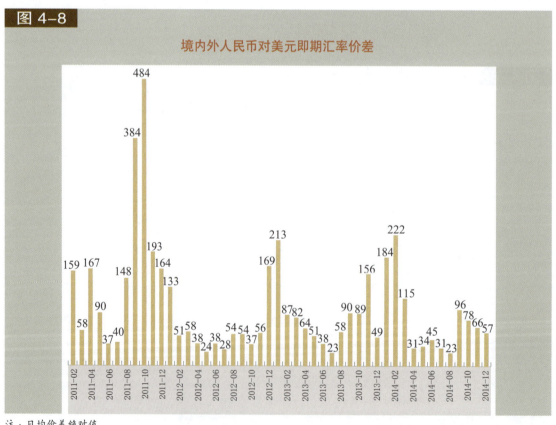

境内外人民币对美元即期汇率价差

注：日均价差绝对值。
数据来源：中国外汇交易中心、路透数据库。

内外市场存在差价是必然现象。但随着跨境人民币业务发展，各类市场主体灵活选择跨境交易的结算货币和买卖外汇的交易地点，推动境内外人民币汇率相互影响、差价收窄。

（二）外汇市场交易

2014 年，国内外汇市场（不含外币对市场）累计成交 12.76 万亿美元（日均521 亿美元），较上年增长 13.4%，增速较上年回落 9.1 个百分点，这反映了当年跨境贸易投资等实体活动放缓，以及离岸人民币外汇市场对在岸市场替代的影响。其中，银行对客户市场和银行间外汇市场分别成交 3.95 万亿美元和 8.81 万亿美元 [1]；即期和衍生产品分别成交 7.25 万亿美元和 5.51 万亿美元（见表 4-1、图 4-9），衍生产品在外汇市场交易总量中的比重升至历史新高的 43.2%。

即期外汇交易小幅增长。 2014 年，即期外汇市场累计成交 7.25 万亿美元，较上年增长 2.3%。在市场分布上，银行对客户即期结售汇（含银行自身，不含远期履约）累计 3.13 万亿美元，较上年增长 3.8%；银行间即期外汇市场累计成交 4.12 万亿美元，较上年增长 1.2%，其中美元交易份额为 94.5%。

远期外汇交易小幅下降。 2014 年，远期外汇市场累计成交 5 979 亿美元，较上

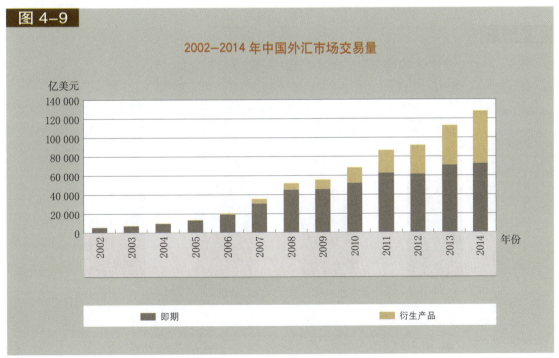

图 4-9

2002—2014 年中国外汇市场交易量

亿美元

（图例）■ 即期　■ 衍生产品

数据来源：国家外汇管理局、中国外汇交易中心。

---

[1] 银行对客户市场采用客户买卖外汇总额，银行间外汇市场采用单边交易量，以下同。

图 4-10

2012-2014 年银行对客户远期结售汇交易量

数据来源：国家外汇管理局。

图 4-11

2014 年银行对客户远期结售汇的交易期限结构

数据来源：国家外汇管理局。

年下降 1.1%。在市场分布上，银行对客户远期结售汇累计签约 5 450 亿美元，其中结汇和售汇分别为 3 005 亿美元和 2 444 亿美元，较上年分别下降 4.7%、下降 14.7% 和增长 11.1%（见图 4-10），6 个月以内的短期交易占 63.4%（见图 4-11）；银行间远期外汇市场累计成交 529 亿美元，较上年增长 63.5%。银行对客户远期交易量下降，除了期权交易的替代效应（期权与远期的交易量比例由 2013 年 9.0% 上升至 2014 年 11.6%）外，突出反映了一些企业的市场风险管理意识薄弱，尚未树立与人民币汇率双向波动相适应的套期保值财务纪律，导致参与衍生产品市场的谨慎心态上升。

外汇和货币掉期交易大幅增长。2014 年，外汇和货币掉期市场累计成交 4.72 万亿美元，较上年增长 35.4%。在市场分布上，银行对客户外汇和货币掉期累计签约 2 173 亿美元，较上年增长 1.7 倍，其中近端结汇 / 远端购汇和近端购汇 / 远端结汇的交易量分别为 192 亿美元和 1 981 亿美元，分别增长 36.3% 和 1.9 倍；银行间外汇和货币掉期市场累计成交 4.50 万亿美元，较上年增长 32.3%。掉期市场持续活跃，表明外汇市场、本外币货币市场之间的内在联系趋于紧密，跨市场资产管理成为一个新趋势。

外汇期权交易大幅增长。2014 年，期权市场累计成交 1 928 亿美元，较上年增长 1.6 倍。在市场分布上，银行对客户期权市场累计成交 629 亿美元，较上年增长 22.3%，3 个月期以内的交易量占比 41.3%；银行间外汇期权市场累计成交 1 299 亿美元，较上年增长 5.0 倍。期权交易大幅增长主要得益于汇改后人民币汇率弹性的增加，以及 2014 年 8 月开始实施的期权发展措施，银行可以为企业更灵活地提供买入或卖出以及组合等多样化期权业务，2014 年 8~12 月期权市场月均交易量较前七个月月均水平增长 3.3 倍。

表 4-1　2014 年中国外汇市场交易概况

交易品种	交易量（亿美元）
即期	72 486
银行对客户市场	31 255
银行间外汇市场	41 232
远期	5 979
银行对客户市场	5 450
其中：3 个月（含）以下	2 540
3 个月至 1 年（含）	2 190
1 年以上	720
银行间外汇市场	529
其中：3 个月（含）以下	392
3 个月至 1 年（含）	132
1 年以上	5
外汇和货币掉期	47 168
银行对客户市场	2 173

续表

交易品种	交易量（亿美元）
银行间外汇市场	44 995
其中：3 个月（含）以下	39 416
3 个月至 1 年（含）	5 424
1 年以上	154
期权	**1 928**
银行对客户市场	**629**
其中：外汇看涨／人民币看跌	333
外汇看跌／人民币看涨	297
其中：3 个月（含）以下	260
3 个月至 1 年（含）	262
1 年以上	108
银行间外汇市场	**1 299**
其中：外汇看涨／人民币看跌	653
外汇看跌／人民币看涨	646
其中：3 个月（含）以下	1 060
3 个月至 1 年（含）	238
1 年以上	1
合计	**127 561**
其中：银行对客户市场	39 507
银行间外汇市场	88 054
其中：即期	72 486
远期	5 979
外汇和货币掉期	47 168
期权	1 928

注：数据均为单边交易额，采用四舍五入原则。
数据来源：国家外汇管理局、中国外汇交易中心。

外汇市场参与者结构基本稳定。银行自营交易延续主导地位（见图 4-12），2014 年银行间交易占整个外汇市场的比重从上年的 66% 上升至 67.7%，非金融客户交易的比重从上年 32.7% 下降至 30.5%，非银行金融机构交易的市场份额较上年上升 0.3 个百分点至 1.7%，非银行金融机构仍是国内外汇市场参与者结构的一个突出短板。

银行间外币对交易下降。2014 年，9 个外币对交易累计成交 606 亿美元，较上年下降 5.7%。其中，即期交易作为最大交易品种累计成交折合 449 亿美元，较上年增长 29.8%，欧元／美元仍是交易量最大的货币对（见图 4-13），其次是美元／港币、澳元／美元交易，三个货币对的交易量占比合计 85.9%。

图 4-12

中国外汇市场的参与者结构

数据来源：国家外汇管理局、中国外汇交易中心。

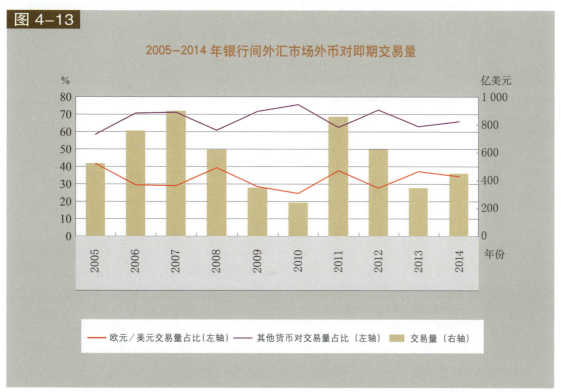

图 4-13

2005—2014 年银行间外汇市场外币对即期交易量

数据来源：中国外汇交易中心。

专栏 5

浅析当前外汇衍生产品套期保值成本

2014年人民币汇率波动性上升，但企业从事外汇衍生产品交易不增反降，4~12月远期结售汇月均签约量较第一季度和2013年全年月均水平分别下降33.4%和15.4%，有观点认为这与当前套期保值成本较高（远期汇率美元升水较多）影响企业积极性有关，但实为误解。

套期保值成本通常可以理解为交易成本和持有成本。交易成本表现为金融产品的买卖价差，价差越宽，投资者在买入与卖出一项金融产品之间所支付的成本越大或者说获取的收益越小。类似期权这种需要单独付费购买的金融工具，期权费也是交易成本。持有成本表现为投资者在交易取得一项金融产品后，因市场价格波动产生市值重估损失而追加抵押担保品或占用更多授信。如果市场价格大幅波动导致投资者的抵押担保品或授信耗尽而无法继续

图 C5-1

境内市场人民币对美元即期和远期汇率

注：1. 即期汇率指银行间外汇市场即期询价收盘汇率。
　　 2. 远期美元升水率＝银行间远期外汇市场美元升水点数／即期汇率。
数据来源：中国外汇交易中心。

持有金融产品，持有成本或者说市值重估损失将转为实际损失。套期保值有交易和持有成本是正常现象，企业成熟、健全的套期保值策略应该是根据自身风险敞口状况和风险承受能力，选择合适的衍生产品进行套期保值，控制风险而非追逐风险。

有的企业从"性价比"角度片面理解套期保值成本。与成熟市场不同，国内一些企业是从开展衍生产品交易是否有利可图的实际财务效果角度理解套期保值成本。例如，企业对于未来出口收入的外汇是选择现在做远期结汇还是未来做即期结汇，是基于比较远期汇率与未来汇率孰高孰低的市场判断，而非控制风险的财务纪律。如果预计远期汇率不比未来汇率高——不省钱或不赚钱，就不保值。这种认识与过去几年的市场环境有关，由于人民币远期汇率反映本外币正利差维持贬值，而即期汇率保持低波动、单边升值，企业做远期结汇几乎稳赚不赔（做远期购汇正好相反），一些企业错误地认为套期保值就该赚钱，忽视了防范汇率波动不确定性的本质功能。

当前人民币汇率已处于均衡水平，双向波动将是一种新常态，企业应该改变以往去看或赌人民币升贬值趋势的交易习惯，建立严格的套期保值财务纪律来管理汇率风险，不能以市场判断来替代市场操作。

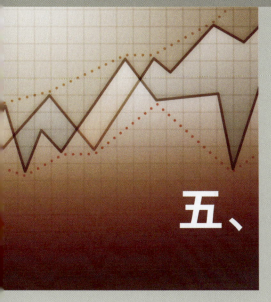

五、国际收支形势
展望

2015 年，预计我国国际收支仍将呈现"经常项目顺差、资本和金融项目双向波动"的新常态。

经常项目将继续保持一定顺差。一方面，随着世界经济尤其是美国经济的持续复苏，有助于稳定我国的出口市场需求，同时国际大宗商品价格维持低位、国内需求继续平稳增长等，可能继续带动进口价格和进口需求回落，我国外贸进出口顺差将有所增加。另一方面，国内居民境外旅游消费和外商投资企业利润汇出持续高企，我国服务贸易和投资收益逆差将继续保持较高水平。综合上述两方面因素的影响，2015 年我国经常项目仍将呈现顺差，但经常项目顺差与国内生产总值之比仍会保持在国际公认的合理范围之内。

跨境资本流动有可能震荡加剧。跨境资本流动易受汇率、利率以及市场预期等因素的综合影响。从外部环境看，美国经济复苏势头良好，不排除 2015 年下半年美联储可能启动加息，带动美元进一步走强。同时，近期国际环境动荡不安，欧债谈判再现波折、地缘政治冲突此起彼伏等，都加剧了全球金融市场动荡，带动国际资本流向美国或投向美元等避险货币，新兴经济体面临资本流出压力。从国内环境看，在国内经济从"三期叠加"向新常态过渡的过程中，市场主体对经济下行、金融和房地产领域风险积聚等因素十分敏感，"资产外币化、对外债务去杠杆化"等资产负债结构调整可能持续。上述因素相互叠加，将在短期内加大资本和金融项目双向波动。

尽管内外部环境中的不稳定、不确定因素依然存在，我国跨境资本流动的波动性可能加大，但国际收支差额有望延续规模适度、总体可控的调整。首先，我国经济增速虽有所回落，但保持在 7% 上下的中高增速。随着改革红利不断释放，我国经济仍存在较大的发展空间。这是人民币汇率、国际收支运行维持基本稳定的重要支撑。其次，货物贸易和直接投资依然是国际收支顺差的稳定来源。随着我国出口产品由劳动密集型转向资本和技术密集型，高铁等重大装备制造业成为了出口的新亮点，我国出口竞争优势依然存在。同时，我国是全球最大的消费市场，随着全面改革措施落地和国内金融市场开放，对外资尤其是长期资本仍具有较强的吸引力。最后，我国外汇储备充裕，抵御外部冲击的能力较强。当然，由于我国经济对外开放度越来越高，跨境资本流动渠道日益丰富且便利，部分领域的跨境套利投机活动也需要密切关注。

专栏 6

新兴市场国家宏观经济政策组合调整的理论与实践

20 世纪 50 年代，加拿大经济学家蒙代尔在研究了当时的国际经济形势之后，提出了著名的"三元悖论"，即货币政策独立性、资本自由流动和汇率稳定这三个政策目标不可能同时实现，最多只能实现其中两个而必须放弃另外一个。但是，"三元悖论"这一理论高度抽象，只是考虑了政策组合中的极端情况，而宏观经济环境的复杂性催生了诸多建立在"三元悖论"基础上的中间选择。本轮金融危机以来，尽管各经济体，特别是新兴市场国家，在涉及货币、财政、资本管制以及汇率调控等方面的刺激措施层出不穷，但这些措施归根结底都是在"三元悖论"理论框架的指引下推行的。

巴西政府和央行在整个危机期间始终坚持了货币政策的独立性，通过积极调整国内利率水平的方式将通胀率维持在了合理范围内。与此同时，交替使用外汇干预和资本管制措施，不断在汇率稳定和资本流动之间动态地寻找平衡点。在危机前期本币币值面临升值压力的时候，通过征收金融资本税这一资本管制方式来维持汇率稳定；而在汇率相对稳定后，逐渐放弃资本管制措施而提高了对于汇率波动的容忍度。

墨西哥在危机前后所选择的政策组合都是以资本的自由流动为核心，当汇率出现大幅波动时，墨西哥央行实行的期权拍卖计划以及直接干预汇率措

图 C6-1

巴西政策组合调整

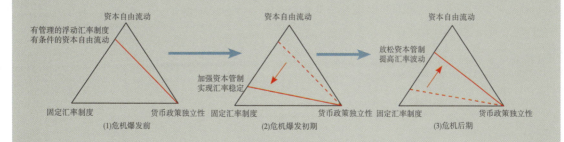

施使货币政策让位于对外汇市场的干预措施，以放弃货币政策独立性为代价来实现汇率水平的稳定；而在汇率稳定后，墨西哥顺势放弃了先前的干预措施，使货币政策重新拥有了独立性地位。因此，我们可以说墨西哥政府和央行的政策组合是不断地在货币政策独立性和稳定的汇率水平之间寻找一个相对均衡点。

图 C6-2

墨西哥政策组合调整

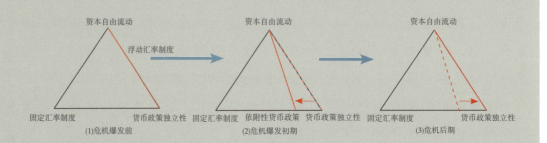

(1)危机爆发前　(2)危机爆发初期　(3)危机后期

从政策组合的角度来看，危机之前俄罗斯致力于将货币政策从外汇管制中剥离出来，立足实现其独立性地位。在危机爆发后，俄罗斯吸取了1998年卢布危机的教训，积极采取措施调控外汇市场，通过牺牲货币政策的方式保证了汇率的稳定。伴随着形势的好转，俄罗斯重新回到力图实现货币政策独立性的轨道上。在"三元悖论"的框架中，俄罗斯的均衡选择始终以资本自由流动为中心，不断在固定汇率制度和货币政策独立性之间进行动态调整。

图 C6-3

俄罗斯政策组合调整

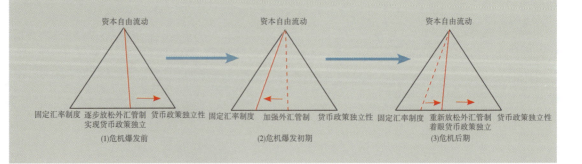

(1)危机爆发前　(2)危机爆发初期　(3)危机后期

通过上述分析我们可以看出，不同于发达国家主要通过压低利率曲线的方式刺激经济复苏，新兴市场国家立足于使用汇率手段应对危机挑战，但是货币政策的独立性始终被明确为政策组合的核心或是长期发展的目标所在，即维持国内价格的稳定是政策组合的首要目的。作为新兴市场国家的一员，我国在现阶段也同样面临着"三元悖论"的难题，需要按照党的十八届三中全会的既定目标，进一步完善人民币汇率市场化形成机制，适应资本市场双向开放以及跨境资本和金融交易可兑换程度的提高，保证货币政策独立性。

2015 年，面对错综复杂的国内外形势，外汇管理部门将更加积极有为、改革创新，主动适应国际收支和外汇形势的新常态，以促进国际收支平衡为目标、以防范跨境资本冲击为前提，按照外汇管理"五个转变"的要求，重点推进人民币资本项目可兑换等关键改革。具体来看：一是深化改革，加快推进人民币资本项目可兑换，积极推进外汇市场发展；二是依法行政，继续推动外汇管理简政放权，促进贸易投资便利化；三是管理转型，加快构建宏观审慎管理框架下的外债和资本流动管理体系，完善政策储备和应对预案；四是加大力度，严厉打击外汇领域违规经营和违法犯罪行为，保持对异常跨境资金流出入的高压态势；五是服务大局，推进外汇储备创新运用，完善外汇储备经营管理。

I. Overview of the Balance of Payments

(I) The Balance-of-Payments Environment

In 2014 China faced complicated and difficult situations both domestically and internationally. The global economy was recovering with twist and turns, and the domestic economy was growing within a reasonable range with increased downward pressures. The two-way floatation of the RMB exchange rate surged remarkably and the balance of payments was moving in the direction of a general equilibrium amidst fluctuations.

Internationally, the global economy maintained a trend of unbalanced recovery, with varying economic performance in the different economies (see Chart 1-1) and a diversified monetary policy in various countries. Economic growth in the United States first declined and then increased, along with the general trend of a strong recovery, and the U.S. employment market was improving. The FED gradually reduced debt purchases and the quantitative easing policy came to the end in October. The Euro zone remained troubled by negative factors, such as deflation and a high unemployment rate, and its economic growth still hovered at a low level. Japan also turned to a negative growth for three quarters beginning with the second quarter. Both the Euro zone and Japan further strengthened their loose monetary policies.

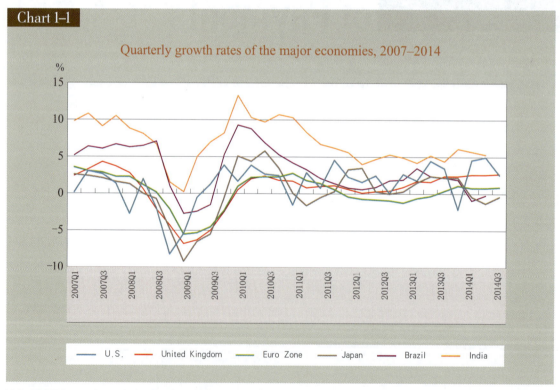

Chart 1-1

Quarterly growth rates of the major economies, 2007–2014

Note: The U.S. growth rate is the annualized quarterly growth; the growth rates of the other countries are the quarterly growth rates year on year.
Source: CEIC.

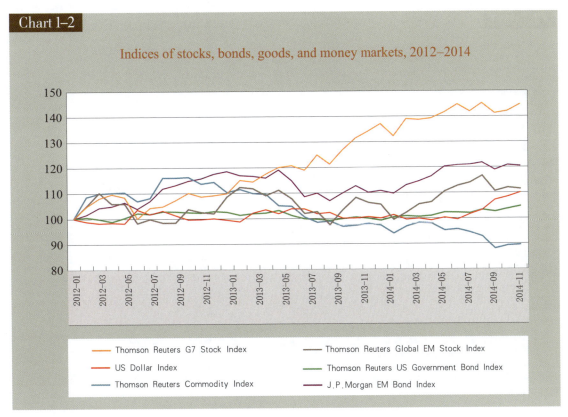

Chart 1–2

Indices of stocks, bonds, goods, and money markets, 2012–2014

— Thomson Reuters G7 Stock Index
— US Dollar Index
— Thomson Reuters Commodity Index
— Thomson Reuters Global EM Stock Index
— Thomson Reuters US Government Bond Index
— J.P.Morgan EM Bond Index

Note: Year 2012=100.
Source: Reuters.

Some emerging economies faced multiple difficulties, such as insufficient endogenous growth, dropping asset prices, and even capital outflows, which forced them to choose between economic stimulation and restraining capital outflows in terms of their monetary policies. More complicated monetary policies and low global growth rates contributed to fluctuations in international financial markets. On the one hand, major stock and bond markets went up, with more significant fluctuations in the second half of the year. On the other hand, the US dollar began to appreciate, whereas the other currencies and prices of staple goods dropped (see Chart 1–2).

Domestically, China's economic and social development was steady, despite some difficulties and challenges. The positive factors were due to the high GDP growth rate, the low CPI (see Chart 1–3), and the steady employment market. In addition, the industrial structure was improved and the share of final consumption expenditure to growth increased (see Chart 1–4). The floating zone of the RMB exchange rate expanded and the elasticity of exchange rate increased, which played a more important role in the balance of payments. However, there were also some negative factors, including weak investment and a lack of new consumption

Chart 1-3

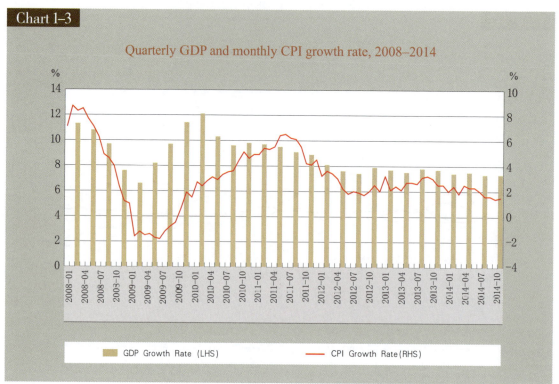

Quarterly GDP and monthly CPI growth rate, 2008–2014

GDP Growth Rate (LHS)   CPI Growth Rate (RHS)

Source: CEIC.

Chart 1-4

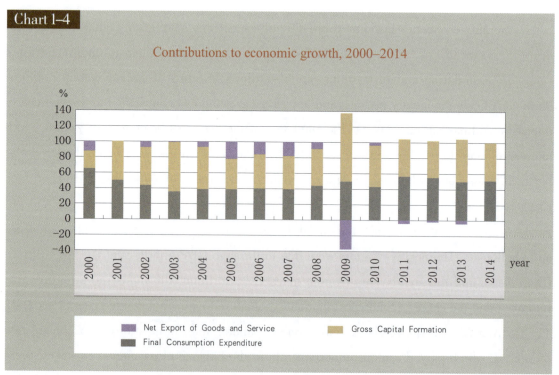

Contributions to economic growth, 2000–2014

Net Export of Goods and Service   Gross Capital Formation
Final Consumption Expenditure

Source: CEIC.

hot spots, making it more difficult to realize steady growth. Against the background that China had to deal simultaneously with the slowdown in economic growth, making difficult structural adjustments, and absorbing the effects of the previous economic stimulus policies, there were potential risks in some areas and market participants accelerated the currency structural adjustments of their assets and liabilities.

(II) The Main Characteristics of the Balance of Payments

The balance of payment recorded a twin surplus. In 2014 the BOP surplus amounted to USD 257.9 billion, down by 48 percent year on year (see Table 1–1). In particular, the current account surplus was USD 219.7 billion, an increase of 48 percent year on year, [1]and the capital and financial account surplus was USD 38.2 billion, a decrease of 89 percent year on year.

The trade in goods surplus grew rapidly. Based on the balance–of–payments statistics, [2]China's exports and imports of trade in goods amounted to USD 2 354.1 billion and USD 1 878.2 billion, up 6 percent and 1 percent respectively, and the surplus was USD 476 billion, up 32 percent year on year (see Chart 1–5).

Table 1-1 The structure of the BOP surplus, 2008–2014   Units: In 100 million USD

Items	2008	2009	2010	2011	2012	2013	2014
BOP balance	4 607	4 417	5 247	4 016	1 836	4 943	2 579
Current account balance	4 206	2 433	2 378	1 361	2 154	1 482	2 197
As a of the BOP balance (%)	91	55	45	34	117	30	85
As a of GDP(%)	9.3	4.9	4.0	1.9	2.6	1.6	2.1
Capital and financial account balance	401	1 985	2 869	2 655	-318	3 461	382
As a of the BOP balance (%)	9	45	55	66	-17	70	15
As a of GDP(%)	0.9	4.0	4.8	3.6	-0.4	3.6	0.4

Source: SAFE, NBS.

---

① In 2013 the BOP was revised according to the latestd data. After the revision, the BOP surplus was USD 494.3 billion. In particular, the current account surplus was USD 148.2 billion, a decrease of USD 34.6 billion from the previous release of the BOP. The capital and financial account surplus was USD 346.1 billion, an increase of USD 19.9 billion from the previous release of the BOP. The major adjustment came from foreign shareholders' accrual profits and unremitted profits based on the annual survey of FDI enterprises, which led to an increase of USD 35.4 billion in both income outflows and FDI inflows.

② The BOP statistics and the statistics of the General Administration of Customs with respect to trade in goods can be reconciled by the following: First, imports based on the BOP statistics equal 95 percent of the imports based on the customs statistics by quoting the CIF and assuming 5 percent to be insurance and freight. Second, the BOP statistics include goods repatriation, goods purchased at ports, and smuggled goods that are deducted from the import and export returns.

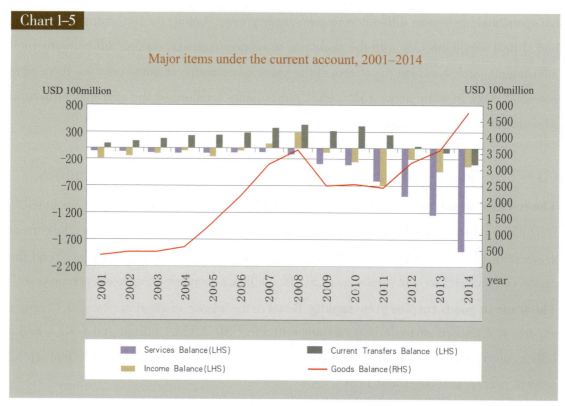

Chart 1-5

Major items under the current account, 2001–2014

Source: SAFE.

The deficit in trade in services continued to expand. In 2014 trade in services revenue totaled USD 190.9 billion, decreasing 7 percent year on year; trade in services expenditures totaled USD 382.9 billion, increasing 16 percent; and the deficit of trade in services was USD 192 billion, an increase of 54 percent, among which the transportation deficit increased by 2 percent and the travel deficit continued to increase at a rate of 40 percent year on year (see Chart 1–5).

The deficit in income decreased. In 2014 income revenue totaled USD 213 billion, up by 16 percent year on year; income expenditures totaled USD 247.1 billion, down by 6 percent; and the deficit was USD 34.1 billion, down by 57 percent. In particular, employee compensation recorded a surplus of USD 25.8 billion, up by 60 percent, and investment income recorded a deficit of USD 59.9 billion, down by 37 percent (see Chart 1–5). However, the deficit in investment income did not represent a loss of China's outward investments. Instead, in 2014 China's outward investments recorded revenue of USD 183.1 billion, an increase of 10 percent year on year. Foreign investment profits and dividend expenditures totaled USD 242.9 billion, down by 7 percent.

The deficit in current transfers surged remarkably. In 2014, current transfer revenue amounted to USD 41.1 billion, decreasing 23 percent year on year; current transfer expenditures totaled USD 71.4 billion, increasing 15 percent year on year; and the current transfer item recorded a deficit of USD 30.2 billion, 2.5 times the deficit in 2013 (see Chart 1–5). Current transfers include donations, compensation, social security, taxes, penalties, and lotteries. Since 2013, current transfers changed from a surplus to a deficit, reflecting the increase in donations from residents to nonresidents due to improvements in resident income.

Net inflows of direct investments decreased slightly. Based on the BOP statistics, the surplus in direct investments totaled USD 208.7 billion, a decrease of 4 percent year on year (see Chart 1–6). In particular, outward direct investments recorded a net outflow of USD 80.4 billion, representing growth of 10 percent, and inward direct investments[①] recorded net inflows of USD 289.1 billion, down by 1 percent.

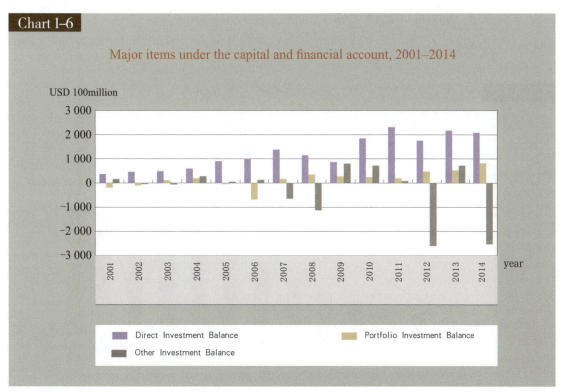

Chart 1–6

Major items under the capital and financial account, 2001–2014

Source: SAFE.

---

① Unlike the data released by the Ministry of Commerce, direct investments based on the BOP statistics also include unpaid and unremitted profits, retained earnings, shareholder loans, foreign capital utilized by financial institutions, and real estate bought by non-residents.

Net inflows of portfolio investments surged. In 2014 net inflows of portfolio investment amounted to USD 82.4 billion, up by 56 percent year on year (see Chart 1–6). In particular, outward portfolio investments recorded a net outflow of USD 10.8 billion, an increase of 102 percent year on year; inward portfolio investments recorded a net inflow of USD 93.2 billion, an increase of 60 percent.

Other investments changed from net inflows to net outflows. In 2014 other investments recorded a net outflow of USD 252.8 billion, whereas in 2013 they had recorded a net inflow of USD 72.2 billion (see Chart 1–6). In particular, assets such as lending, trade credits, and deposits recorded a net increase of USD 303 billion, up by 113 percent year on year. Liabilities such as debts, trade credits, and deposits recorded a net increase of USD 50.2 billion, down by 77 percent.

The growth rate of reserve assets slowed down. The increase in reserve assets in 2014 totaled USD 117.8 billion, a decrease of 73 percent year on year. In particular, foreign reserve assets increased USD 118.8 billion, which represented a decreased growth rate of 73 percent year on year. By the end of 2014, China's foreign reserve position was USD 3 843 billion (see Chart 1–7), an increase by USD 21.7 billion from its position in 2013 and a decrease of USD

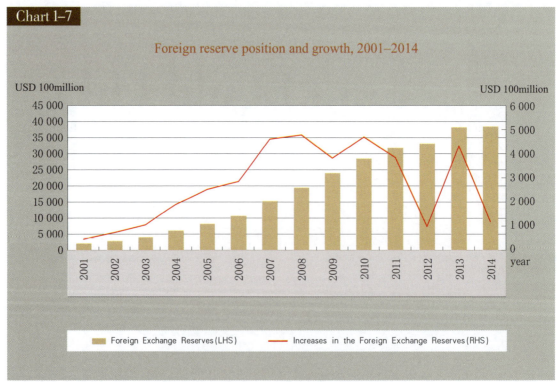

Chart 1–7

Foreign reserve position and growth, 2001–2014

Note: The increase in foreign reserves is driven by transactions, but excluding the valuation effect.
Source: SAFE.

488 billion compared with the increase in 2013. The increase in the foreign reserve position was USD 97.1 billion less than the increase in foreign reserve assets, reflecting the valuation effects without cross–border capital flows due to the exchange fluctuations in the major currencies as well as the asset prices in international markets.

Table 1-2 China's balance of payments statement in 2014[①]

Unit: USD 100 million

Item	Balance	Credit	Debit
I. Current account	**2 197**	**27 992**	**25 795**
A. Goods and services	2 840	25 451	22 611
a. Goods	4 760	23 541	18 782
b. Services	-1 920	1 909	3 829
1.Transportation	-579	382	962
2.Travel	-1 079	569	1 649
3.Communication services	-5	18	23
4.Construction services	105	154	49
5. Insurance services	-179	46	225
6. Financial services	-4	45	49
7.Computer and information services	99	184	85
8. Royalties and licensing fees	-219	7	226
9. Consulting services	164	429	265
10. Advertising and public opinion polling	12	50	38
11. Audio-visual and related services	-7	2	9
12.Other business services	-217	14	231
13. Government services, n.i.e.	-10	11	20
B. Income	-341	2 130	2 471
1.Compensation of employees	258	299	42
2.Investment income	-599	1 831	2 429
C. Current transfers	-302	411	714
1.General government	-29	16	46
2.Other sectors	-273	395	668
II. Capital and financial account	**382**	**25 730**	**25 347**
A. Capital account	0	19	20
B. Financial account	383	25 710	25 328

---

① China's balance of payments statement is compiled in accordance with the principles of the fifth edition of the *Balance of Payments Manual* of the International Monetary Fund, recording all economic transactions between residents of the Chinese mainland (excluding residents of Hong Kong SAR, Macau SAR, and Taiwan province) and non–residents, based on the principles of a double–entry system.

(Gontinued)

Item	Balance	Credit	Debit
1. Direct investment	2 087	4 352	2 266
1.1 Abroad	-804	555	1 359
1.2 In China	2 891	3 797	906
2. Portfolio investment	824	1 664	840
2.1 Assets	-108	293	401
2.1.1 Equity securities	-14	170	184
2.1.2 Debt securities	-94	123	217
2.1.2.1 Bonds and notes	-92	123	215
2.1.2.2 Money market instruments	-2	0	2
2.2 Liabilities	932	1 371	439
2.2.1 Equity securities	519	777	258
2.2.2 Debt securities	413	594	181
2.2.2.1 Bonds and notes	410	497	88
2.2.2.2 Money market instruments	4	97	94
3. Other investment	-2 528	19 694	22 222
3.1 Assets	-3 030	995	4 025
3.1.1 Trade credits	-688	282	970
Long-term	-14	6	19
Short-term	-674	276	950
3.1.2 Loans	-738	177	915
Long-term	-455	0	455
Short-term	-282	177	459
3.1.3 Currency and deposits	-1 597	514	2 111
3.1.4 Other assets	-8	22	29
Long-term	0	0	0
Short-term	-8	22	29
3.2 Liabilities	502	18 699	18 197
3.2.1 Trade credits	-21	154	174
Long-term	0	3	3
Short-term	-20	151	171
3.2.2 Loans	-343	17 464	17 807
Long-term	-57	511	569
Short-term	-286	16 953	17 239
3.2.3 Currency and deposits	814	994	180
3.2.4 Other liabilities	52	87	35
Long-term	58	64	6
Short-term	-6	23	29
III. Reserve assets	**-1 178**	**312**	**1 490**
3.1 Monetary gold	0	0	0
3.2 Special drawing rights	1	1	1
3.3 Reserve position in the fund	10	13	4
3.4 Foreign exchange	-1 188	298	1 486
3.5 Other claims	0	0	0
IV. Net errors and omissions	**-1 401**	**0**	**1 401**

Source: SAFE.

Negative net errors and omissions do not represent capital flight

"Net errors and omissions" is a common feature in the balance of payments for every economy. According to international standards, compilation of the balance of payments should follow the double–entry accounting principle. To make the credits always equal to the debits, an item called the "net errors and omissions" was created in the balance of payments. In China, the compilers use not only the major source data, data from the international–transaction–reporting–system (ITRS), but also supplementary data from Customs, People's Bank of China, and China National Tourism Administration to compile the BOP. Because the data of other government departments and statistical systems may deviate from the BOP concepts, coverage, and recording principles, and because some types of transactions cannot be fully recorded in the departmental statistics, errors and omissions in China's balance of payments cannot be avoided at the aggregate level.

China's errors and omissions are always within a reasonable range. According to international conventions, the size of the net errors and omissions usually should not exceed positive or negative 5 percent of the total exports and imports of goods in the BOP statement during the same period. As the volume of international transactions expands, the absolute value of the net errors and omissions will increase correspondingly, and high–frequency data tend to have larger errors than low–frequency data. From 2008 to 2013, the ratio of net errors and omissions to total exports and imports of goods in China's BOP was approximately 2 percent each year. In 2014, the ratio increased to 5.6 percent and 5.9 percent in the third and fourth quarters respectively, but the annual ratio decreased to 3.3 percent (see Chart C1–1). In the advanced economies, there are also "net errors and omissions" in the BOP statements. For example, in the Q2 2014 U.S. balance of payments, the current account deficit totaled USD 103.5 billion, the capital account surplus totaled USD 10.3 billion, the reserve assets increased by USD 0.8 billion, and the net errors and omissions recorded a positive USD 94 billion. As a result, the ratio of net errors and omissions to total exports and imports of goods in the second quarter of 2014 was 9 percent. More strikingly, the ratio rockets to 15 percent in the first quarter of 2012.

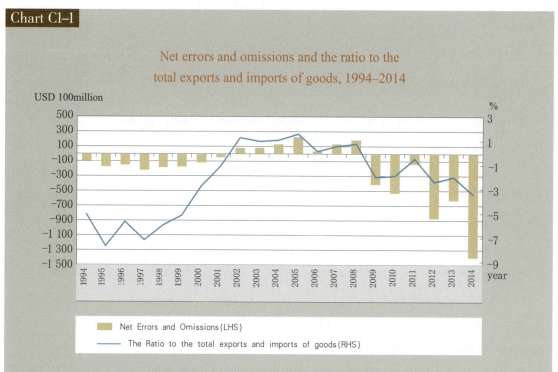

Chart C1-1

Net errors and omissions and the ratio to the
total exports and imports of goods, 1994–2014

Net Errors and Omissions (LHS)
The Ratio to the total exports and imports of goods (RHS)

Source: SAFE.

Negative net errors and omissions do not equal capital flight. First, the direction of the net errors and omissions is not necessarily linked to the direction of the cross–border capital flows. From 2009 to 2013, China's annual balance of payments recorded negative net errors and omissions for four consecutive years. However, during the same period except for 2012, China mainly faced capital inflows and RMB appreciation pressures. Internationally, Japan recorded positive net errors and omissions from 2007 to 2012, as did Germany from 2003 to 2009. But both economies experienced exchange rate appreciations and depreciations, as well as large macroeconomic fluctuations during the same periods (see Chart C1–2). Second, negative errors and omissions are due to various complex reasons. They may arise either because we underestimate the capital outflows or because we overestimate the current account surplus. Such incentive mechanisms as FDI policies of "rewarding exports and constraining imports" in the foreign trade sector and the "tolerance of inflows and intolerance of outflows" may be the underlying reasons. In recent years, the SAFE's inspections have identified that some exporters did not collect, or collected fewer, export proceeds from abroad. The inspections also found that some enterprises claimed larger exports for more government rewards or illegally retained their exports proceeds abroad. Moreover, compared with the increasingly complete external debts statistics, the

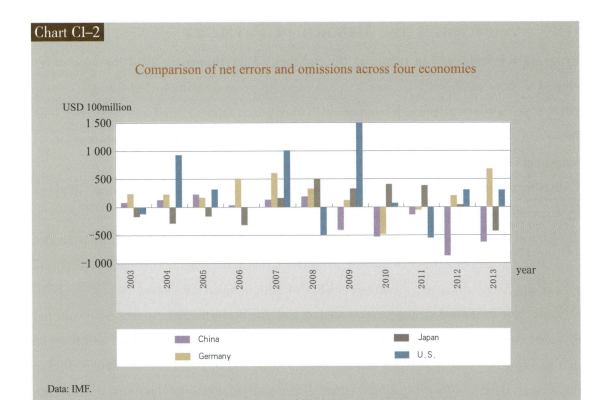

Chart C1-2

Comparison of net errors and omissions across four economies

Data: IMF.

statistics on external claims are relatively weak. As a result, there may outflows of some unclaimed capital not because they are illegal, but because the current system does not accurately record them.

The authorities are managing to improve quality of BOP data. Under the circumstances that new questions and new situations are emerging every day, the SAFE is managing to decrease the size of the net errors and omissions by continuously improving the statistical methodology. For example, the SAFE has launched a new *Report on External Assets, Liabilities, and Transactions*, which collects not only the external assets and liabilities of the reporters, but also the transactions and non–transaction flows of the external positions. To separately identify non–transaction flows is a key step to control their impact on the quality of the BOP. Meanwhile, to improve the statistics on international travel expenses, the report has started to collect cross–border consumption and cash withdrawals via domestic bankcard. Moreover, in addition to the current enterprise survey and the transaction–by–transaction data reporting system, the SAFE is studying sample surveys and estimate methods, so that it can compile more complete, accurate, and reliable BOP data at lower costs.

(III) Evaluation of the Balance of Payments

Progress was achieved in terms of the balance of payments. In 2014 the ratio of the current account surplus to GDP was 2.1 percent, 0.5 percentage point higher than the ratio in 2013, which was consistent with internationally recognized rational standards (see Chart 1–8). Reserve assets based on the BOP statistics increased USD 117.8 billion, accounting for 1.1 percent of GDP, a drop of 3.4 percentage points year on year.

Cross-border capital flows experienced surging fluctuations. Though China's balance of payments recorded a twin surplus for both the current account and the capital account in 2014, cross–border capital flows were changing between surpluses and deficits from quarter to quarter. In particular, the first quarter, as in 2013, registered a net inflow and the surplus of capital and financial account amounted to USD 94 billion. Since the second quarter, the RMB exchange rate fluctuated significantly as well as both the domestic and external economic and financial environments, which led to higher pressures of cross–border outflows and resulted in a situation of a current account surplus and a capital and financial account deficit. During the second, third and fourth quarters, although the trade in goods surplus expanded and the current account surplus increased, the capital and financial account recorded a deficit of USD

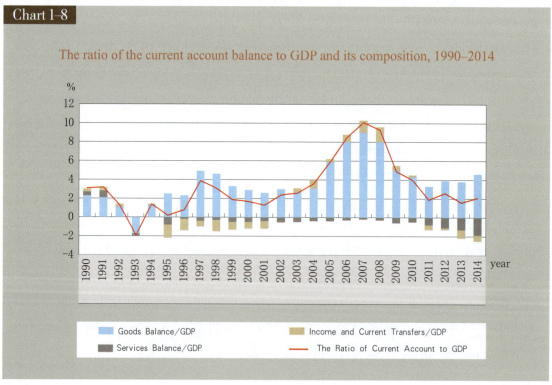

Chart 1–8

The ratio of the current account balance to GDP and its composition, 1990–2014

Legend:
- Goods Balance/GDP
- Services Balance/GDP
- Income and Current Transfers/GDP
- The Ratio of Current Account to GDP

Sources: SAFE, NBS.

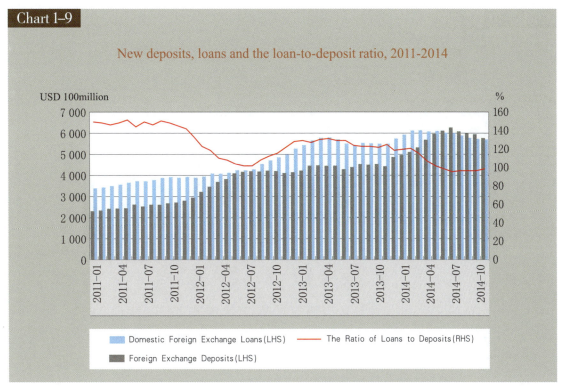

Chart 1-9

New deposits, loans and the loan-to-deposit ratio, 2011-2014

Domestic Foreign Exchange Loans(LHS)   — The Ratio of Loans to Deposits(RHS)
Foreign Exchange Deposits(LHS)

Source: PBC.

16.2 billion, USD 9 billion, and USD 30.5 billion respectively.

The major ways to distribute foreign exchange are to encourage holding of foreign exchange by the people and repayment of the debt. Against the background that RMB exchange rate was moving in the direction of an equilibrium and remarkably fluctuating both upward and downward, domestic enterprises and individuals adjusted and optimized their balance sheets. In 2014, newly increased foreign exchange deposits amounted to USD 108.4 billion, and newly increases foreign exchange loans amounted to USD 20.4 billion (see Chart 1–9). The difference between foreign exchange deposits and loans was utilized by banks in foreign markets, which became the major source of remarkably increased external lending and deposits under other investment assets. Foreign assets holdings were diversified among market participants instead of only by the government, whereas they were controlled by domestic entities. Meanwhile, other investment liabilities recorded net inflows of USD 50.2 billion, a drop in the growth rate by 77 percent year on year, reflecting that domestic enterprises had accelerated their repayment of the USD debt. In 2014, outstanding cross–border borrowing for imports decreased by USD 44.9 billion, whereas in 2013 it had increased by USD 102.7 billion (see Chart 1–10).

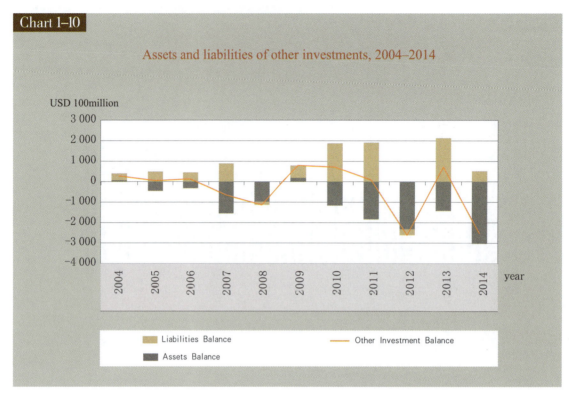

Chart 1–10

Assets and liabilities of other investments, 2004–2014

USD 100million

Source: SAFE.

The BOP adjustment was predictable and acceptable. Along with the reform of the market−oriented RMB exchange rate mechanism, the central bank gradually exited from its normal intervention in the foreign exchange market, which certainly led to an increased trade surplus and more capital outflows. Moreover, more foreign exchange held by the people reflected a growing desire among market participants to hold foreign exchange, which was consistent with the government's reform goal in favor of promoting a foreign exchange supply and demand equilibrium and improving macro controls. Debt deleveraging helped enterprises to relieve the currency mismatches as well as to better face capital flow shocks. More importantly, increased capital outflow pressures since the second quarter did not change the situation of the BOP twin surplus situation for the whole year. Foreign reserve assets continued to increase, with the growth rate 20 percent higher than the growth rate in 2012 when the outflow pressures were also high.

II.Analysis of the Major Items in the Balance of Payments

(I) Trade in goods

According to statistics of the General Administration of Customs, trade in goods in 2014 was characterized as the following.

Decelerated growth of both imports and exports. In 2014, the total of China's imports and exports grew by 3.4 percent year on year, lower than the growth rate in 2013 (7.6 percent). In particular, exports and imports grew by 6.1 percent and 0.4 percent respectively. The major reasons for the deceleration were weak domestic demand and the drop in the prices of staple goods as well as high trade record in 2013 which was driven by arbitrage trade. According to the estimation of the Ministry of Commerce.[1]after excluding the influence from arbitrage trade in 2013, total exports and imports in 2014 grew by 6.1 percent year on year, among which exports and imports grew by 8.7 percent and 3.3 percent respectively in real terms. Foreign trade dependence (the sum of imports and exports/GDP) further fell to 42 percent, 3 percentage points lower than that in 2013 and 23 percentage points lower than the historical high ratio in 2006 (see Chart 2–1), which indicated the enhanced endogeneity of China's economic growth.

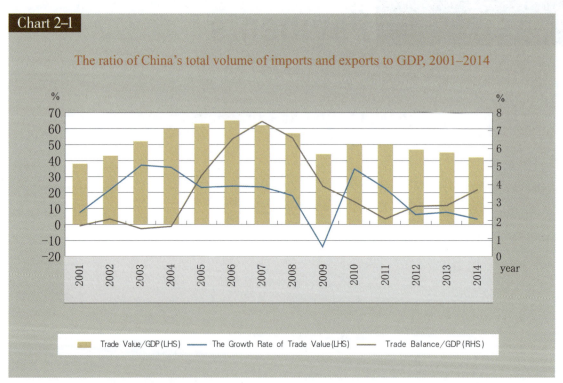

Chart 2–1

The ratio of China's total volume of imports and exports to GDP, 2001–2014

Trade Value/GDP(LHS) — The Growth Rate of Trade Value(LHS) — Trade Balance/GDP(RHS)

Sources: General Administration of Customs, NBS.

---

[1] See detailed information on the conventional news release by the Ministry of Commerce on January, 21, 2015.

Expanded surplus in trade in goods. In 2014 the surplus in trade in goods amounted to USD 382.5 billion, growth of 47.3 percent year on year. The main reason for the increased surplus was due to the decrease in import prices. Under the circumstances of dropping prices for both domestic industrial products and staple goods in international markets, the import price index for 2014 declined by 3.3 percent year on year. In particular, the volume of crude oil imports grew by 9.5 percent whereas imports grew by only 3.9 percent; the volume of iron ore imports grew by 13.8 percent whereas imports declined by 11.8 percent; and the volume of coal and lignite coal imports decreased by 10.9 percent whereas imports declined by 23.5 percent. Factors such as decelerated growth of domestic demand and decreased trade financing of staple goods influenced the import growth. In 2014, nominal fixed-asset investments increased by 15.7 percent year on year, 3.9 percentage points lower than the growth rate in 2013. For instance, the ratio of trade financing of copper was 89 percent in the first quarter of 2013, but the ratio dropped remarkably in the second half of 2014, with a ratio of 2 percent in the third quarter and a negative ratio in the fourth quarter. The government does not intend to pursue the goal of surplus expansion. However, objectively speaking, the increased surplus did strengthen the capability to protect against capital flow shocks. The ratio of the surplus of trade in goods to GDP was 3.7 percent, higher than the ratio during the previous two years (see Chart 2–1).

Improved trade structure. In terms of trade patterns, ordinary trade accounted for 53.8 percent of total trade, which was 1 percentage points higher than the ratio in 2013 and marked an increase for two consecutive years. The contribution of processing trade fell further to 32.8 percent, far less than the ratio in 2005 (nearly 50 percent) (see Chart 2–2). In terms of trade participants, private enterprises accounted for over 70 percent of the total participants, 1.6 percentage points more than the ratio in 2013. Trade in goods of private enterprises accounted for 36.5 percent of the total trade, 0.6 percentage point higher than the ratio in 2013. With respect to the increased trade in goods, private enterprises accounted for 55.9 percent of the total, indicating that they had become a major source of the growth in trade in goods (see Chart 2–3).

More diversified trade partners. The ratio of trade with the developing countries increased 0.4 percentage point year on year. In particular, the growth rate of trade with EMEAP, India, Russia, Africa, and the Middle Eastern European countries was higher than the average rates. Trade with the advanced countries remained stable. Trade with the European Union and the United States grew by 9.9 percent and 6.6 percent year on year. Despite the deceleration in the growth rate, it was still higher than the projected global rate and China remained the largest

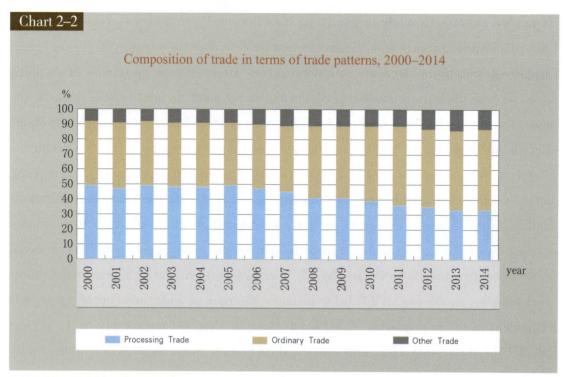

Source: General Administration of Customs.

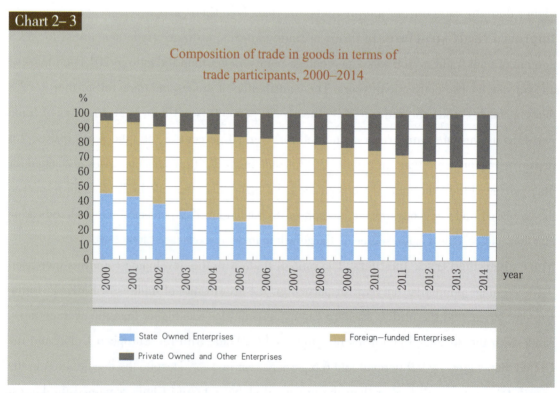

Source: General Administration of Customs.

trade in goods country. In 2014 China's market share among its major trade partners, including the United States, the European Union, and Japan, grew slightly, increasing by 0.5 percentage point, 1.4 percentage points, and 0.6 percentage point respectively, and China's share in the export market rebounded for two successive years.

Box 2

Rapid development of cross–border receipts and payments of e–commerce driven by overseas online shopping

Cross–border e–commerce began to be a new growth engine of foreign trade, with the prevalence of overseas online shopping in China. To adapt to this development, the SAFE launched a foreign exchange pilot policy for cross–border e–commerce payments for payment institutions. The policy aimed to facilitate cross–border e–commerce receipts and payments of foreign exchange. In 2014, there were 22 institutions participating in the pilot program and the receipts and payments via the pilot program grew rapidly.

Cross-border online shopping by individuals was surging. In 2014 the sum of receipts and payments of e–commerce business by payment institutions via the pilot program amounted to USD 1.7 billion. Chinese individuals were actively involved in cross–border online shopping. Individual cross–border online shopping, including payment of individual trade in services, totaled USD 1.5 billion, accounting for 88.5 percent of the total receipts and payments. Due to the cooperation of Chinese payment institutions and overseas major retail online shops such as the Macy's, more and more Chinese tried overseas online shopping, which led to increasing payments for cross–border online shopping. In November and December, in particular, driven by sales due to Western holidays and domestic online shopping, individual cross–border online shopping totaled over 0.2 billion per month for consecutive two months.

The privileges of trade in services form cross-border e-commerce gradually emerged. To ensure the authenticity of transactions, the trade in goods and part of the trade in services with real backgrounds are included in the pilot program. In the first half–year of 2014, trade in goods totaled more than trade in services, but in the third quarter trade in services surpassed trade in goods, although in the fourth quarter trade in goods again exceeded trade in services due to the increase in cross–border online shopping since

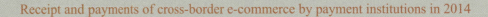

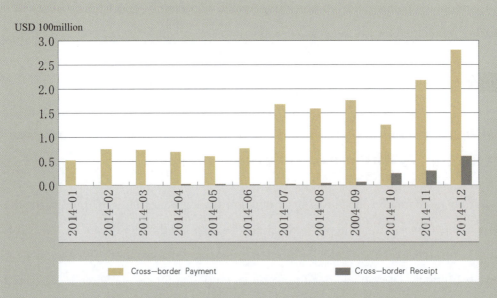

Chart C2-1

Receipt and payments of cross-border e-commerce by payment institutions in 2014

Sources: SAFE.

the last quarter during the traditional hot season for shopping. During the entire year, trade in goods accounted for 56.3 percent of the total. In general, trade in goods accounted for more than trade in services, but the privileges of trade in services via e-commerce were emerging and the amount of trade in services in the fourth quarter grew by 6 percentage more than that in the first quarter.

The pilot business showed an unbalanced trend of development. The pilot business concentrated on only a few payment institutions. A very few institutions dominated in the trade in services and the businesses of many institutions remained underdeveloped. Meanwhile, the privileges of imports over exports were popular and foreign exchange payments dominated the pilot business. Payment institutions had to develop the overseas markets so to introduce foreign consumers to China.

To facilitate the development of cross-border e-commerce, the SAFE released the *Notice on the Pilot Program on Cross-Border Foreign Exchange Payments and Receipt by Payment Institutions* in January 2015, allowing qualified payment institutions to participate on the pilot program and increasing the upper limit for single receipts or payments and expanding the business coverage.

(II) Trade in services

Trade in services continued to grow steadily and there was significant growth in high value-added trade in. In 2014 trade in services amounted to USD 573.8 billion, a growth rate of 7 percent year on year, which was 3 percentage points higher than the growth rate for trade in goods. Trade in services accounted for 14 percent of total trade in goods, 0.4 percentage point higher than the ratio in 2013 (see Chart 2–4). According to the WTO *World Trade Report*, in 2004 the ratio of China's trade in services to that in the United States, Germany, and the United Kingdom was 22 percent, 40 percent, and 42 percent respectively, whereas in 2013, the ratio had been 49 percent, 88 percent, and 114 percent respectively, indicating that China's trade in services was developing rapidly and the differences between China and the advanced countries were narrowing. Guided by the government's policy to optimize the structure of trade in services, high value–added trade in services realized rapid development. In 2014, financial services, communications services, construction services, and computer and information services grew by 38 percent, 24 percent, 38 percent, and 25 percent respectively year on year, whereas transportation, as a traditional trade in services, grew by only 2 percent.

Receipts from trade in services recorded a historical low level during the last five years. In 2014 receipts from trade in services amounted to USD 190.9 billion, dropping by 7 percent

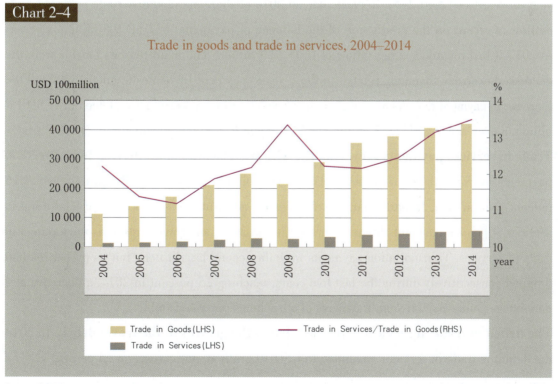

Chart 2–4

Trade in goods and trade in services, 2004–2014

Source: SAFE.

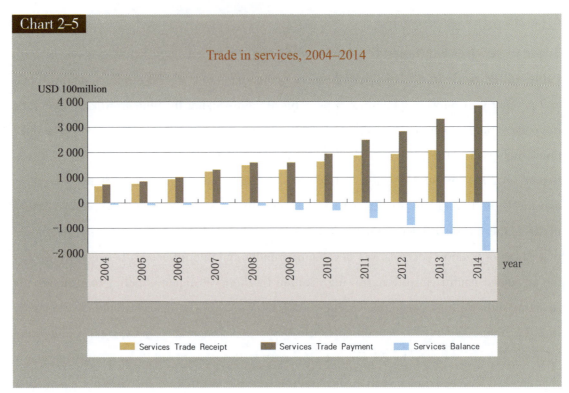

Chart 2–5

Trade in services, 2004–2014

USD 100million

Legend: Services Trade Receipt, Services Trade Payment, Services Balance

Source: SAFE.

year on year (see Chart 2–5). In particular, in 2014 offshore merchandise trade recorded a net outflow (a record on the credit side of the balance of payments) of USD 9.5 billion, whereas in 2013 it had recorded a net inflow of USD 22.3 billion. The main reasons for this were the decreased overseas financing related to the delayed payment by domestic enterprises and the increase in payment due. As a result, receipts from other business services totaled only USD 1.4 billion, a decrease of USD 32.7 billion and 96 percent lower than the amount in 2013.

Trade in services payments grew rapidly, with travel as the main driving force. In 2014, payments for trade in services totaled USD 382.9 billion (see Chart 2–5), an increase of 16 percent year on year. In particular, travel payments accounted for 43 percent of total trade in services, 4 percentage points higher than the ratio in 2013, and travel ranked as the top item in trade in services. Transportation payments were the second largest item, but its proportion had dropped consecutively during the last five years, reaching 25 percent in 2014, a decrease of 4 percentage points year on year. Payments of other items remained stable.

The deficit in trade in services expanded due to the growth in the travel deficit. In 2014 the deficit in trade in services amounted to USD 192 billion, an increase of 54 percent year on year. Travel accounted for nearly 40 percent of trade in services and was the major source for

Chart 2–6

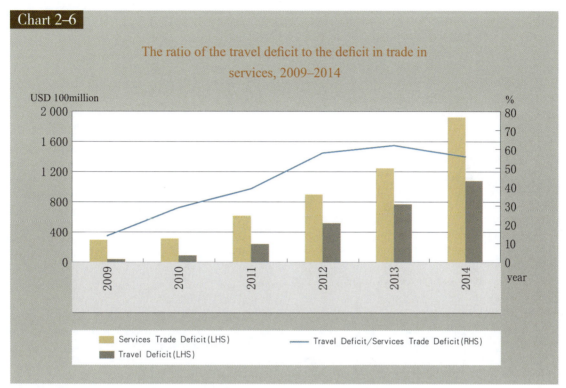

The ratio of the travel deficit to the deficit in trade in services, 2009–2014

Source: SAFE.

the increase in the deficit in trade in services (see Chart 2–6). Due to the increased disposable income, both the population involved in outbound travel and study and the average expenditure per person grew remarkably. In 2014 travel payments totaled USD 164.9 billion, an increase of 28 percent, and travel receipts totaled USD 56.9 billion, an increase of 10 percent. The travel deficit amounted to USD 107.9 billion, a growth rate of 40 percent year on year, accounting for 56 percent of the total deficit in trade in services.

The concentration of the geographic distribution of the deficit trading partners relived but the surplus in trade in services still focused on Hong Kong. In 2014 China recorded a deficit of USD 24.5 billion, with its top ten trading partners with respect to trade in services, decreasing 18 percent year on year. The deficit with the top ten deficit economies totaled USD 75.1 billion, accounting for 40 percent of the total deficit in trade in services, down 20 percentage points year on year. In 2014, the largest deficit economies were the United States, Singapore, Korea, and Australia, and the respective deficits totaled USD 17.1 billion, 10.6 billion, USD 9.7 billion and USD 9.4 billion. The surplus with Hong Kong SAR was USD 43.3 billion, up by 36 percent and accounting for 93 percent of the surplus with the economies with which China held a surplus (see Chart 2–7).

Chart 2-7

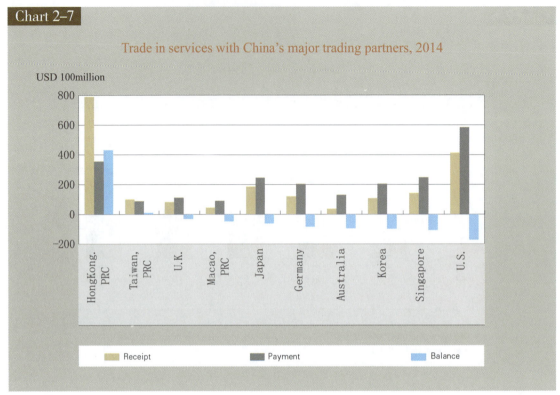

Trade in services with China's major trading partners, 2014

Source: SAFE.

Box 3

Trade in services receipts and payments were generally normal

Trade in services has recorded a long history of deficits, which indicated relative underdevelopment and structural problems in China's trade in services. In 2014, attracting popular attention, the deficit in trade in services increased by USD 67.5 billion to reach a total of USD 192 billion. In fact, China's trade in services has been in deficit since 1995 with the deficit expanding in the more recent years. The growth rate in the deficit of trade in services was 98 percent in 2011. The deficit in trade in services over the long term reflected that China remained relatively weak competitively and lacked a comparative advantage with respect to trade in services in international markets. China's trade in services was relatively underdeveloped compared with its trade in goods, and the ratio of trade in services to trade in goods remained low for a long period of time. This ratio was recorded at one-seventh, whereas the average ratio in the developed countries was recorded at one-third. More significant was the underdevelopment in high value-added services.

The increased deficit in trade in services in recent years reflected upgraded consumption due to the enhanced income of residents. Driven by ever-increasing resident income and the strong RMB exchange rate, residents' overseas purchasing power was improving remarkably, and demand was surging due to the decreased costs for outbound travel, overseas study, and overseas online shopping. In recent years, the number of China's outbound tourists grew rapidly, totaling over 100 million persons in 2014 for the first time, a growth of 18 percent year on year (see Chart C3–1). Increased outbound tourists and their consumption led to continuous increases in travel payments. According to the statistics of the World Tourism Organization of the United Nations, China has been the top country for international tourism consumption since 2012. In 2013, China's outbound tourism consumption amounted to USD 129 billion, which was USD 42 billion more than U.S, consumption, it represented growth of 26 percent from 2013 which had increased by 40 percent year on year. Domestic residents have been enjoying the benefits from the reform and opening up strategy.

The facilitating measures increased trade in services payments, especially with respect to outbound tourism. With the rapid opening up and strengthened national

Chart C3–1

Inbound and outbound tourism, 2001-2014

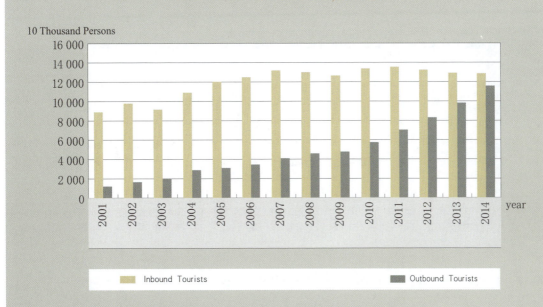

10 Thousand Persons

Inbound Tourists   Outbound Tourists

Source: China National Tourism Administration.

power, the destinations of Chinese residents' outbound tourism continued to increase and many countries and regions introduced preferential policies, such as visa–free policies, visas on arrival, and private tour to attract Chinese tourists. Related foreign exchange reforms, including enhanced limits on individual foreign exchange purchases, simplified approval procedures, and overseas consumption via credit cards and third party payment institutions, and guaranteed foreign exchange purchases of overseas consumption via credit cards were introduced . In the meantime, the SAFE implemented measures to prevent cross–border capital flow risks. For instance, when necessary single receipts or payments over USD 50 000 had to be reviewed with transaction documents and were subject to on–the–spot verifications and reviews.

The deficit in trade in services was favorable for the balance-of-payment macro-control targets. In 2014, according to the BOP statistics, the surplus in trade in goods increased by 32 percent year on year, but its increase was offset by the expanded deficit in trade in services. The total surplus of trade in goods and services was USD 284 billion, the growth rate of which decreased to 21 percent year on year, and the ratio of the surplus to GDP was 2.7 percent. The current account surplus was reasonable (see Chart C3–2).

Chart C3–2

The ratio of the balance trade in goods and services to GDP, 1994-2014

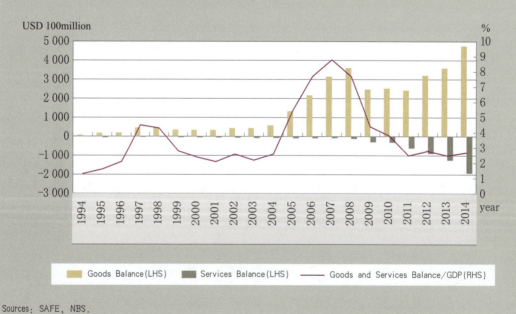

Sources: SAFE, NBS.

(III) Direct investments

Net inflows of direct investments decreased slightly. In 2014, according to the balance–of–payment statistics, direct investment inflows and outflows totaled USD 435.2 billion and USD 226.6 billion respectively, growing by 14 percent and 39 percent year on year. Direct investment net inflows totaled USD 208.7 billion, down by 4 percent. In 2014, the sum of the current account balance and the direct investment balance (i.e., the basic BOP balance) was USD 428.4 billion, growing by 17 percent year on year and accounting for 4.1 percent of GDP, which was an increase of 0.3 percentage point from the ratio in 2013. China was further strengthened against capital flow shocks (see Chart 2–8).

Net inflows of inward direct investments (FDI) remained stable. In 2014, net inflows of FDI totaled USD 289.1 billion, decreasing 1 percent year on year (see Chart 2–9). FDI inflows amounted to USD 379.7 billion, up by 10 percent. In particular, equity investment inflows totaled USD 145.6 billion, profit reinvestment inflows totaled USD 129.2 billion, and other capital inflows (including loans and C/A payments between foreign–funded enterprises and their overseas affiliates) totaled USD 104.9 billion, an increase of 4 percent, a decrease of 10 percent, and an increase of 72 percent year on year respectively. FDI outflows totaled

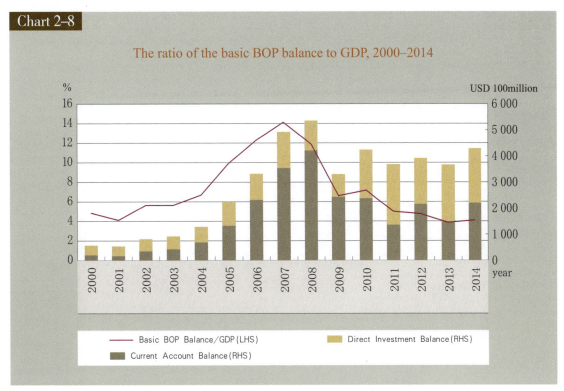

Chart 2–8

The ratio of the basic BOP balance to GDP, 2000–2014

Basic BOP Balance/GDP (LHS)
Direct Investment Balance (RHS)
Current Account Balance (RHS)

Sources: SAFE, NBS.

USD 90.6 billion, up by 70 percent year on year. In particular, the outflow of loans and C/A payments with overseas affiliates totaled USD 73.4 billion, up by 107 percent. Under the circumstance that China had to deal simultaneously with the slowdown in economic growth, to make difficult structural adjustments, and to absorb the effects of the previous economic stimulus policies, foreign capital was still confident about long–term investment in China. In addition, the difference between the domestic and foreign markets regarding the financing environment and the impact of costs on the financial behavior of domestic enterprises with their overseas affiliates (see the 2014 *Monitoring Report on China's Cross–Border Capital Flows*, part 2, direct investments).

Outward direct investments (ODI) continued to grow rapidly. In 2014 ODI outflows and inflows amounted to USD 135.9 billion and USD 55.5 billion respectively, growing by 24 percent and 53 percent year on year and reaching a net outflow of USD 80.4 billion, or growth of 10 percent (see Chart 2–10). In terms of sectors, the financial sector recorded a net ODI outflow of USD 11.6 billion, down by 26 percent year on year, with the main source from the banking sector where overseas equity investment decreased by 46 percent to USD 3.3 billion. Net outflows of the non–financial sector totaled USD 68.9 billion, up by 20 percent, reflecting that Chinese enterprises were going out rapidly with relatively concentrated industries and

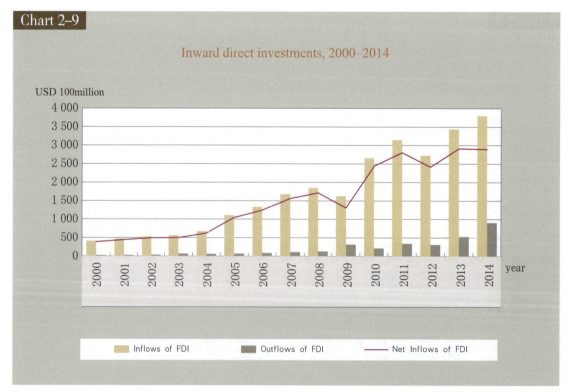

Chart 2–9

Inward direct investments, 2000–2014

Source: SAFE.

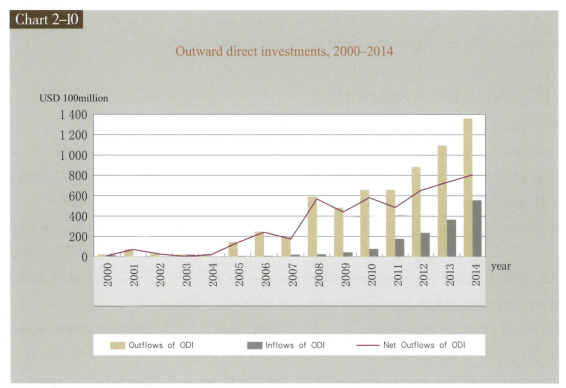

Chart 2–10

Outward direct investments, 2000–2014

Source: SAFE.

destinations (see Chart 2–11). Mergers and acquisitions by domestic enterprises in overseas market were developing significantly. In 2014 Chinese enterprises were actively involved in mergers and acquisitions in industries such as energy and mining, manufacturing, and agriculture. For instance, the enterprise consortium with MMG Limited acquired Las Bambas in Peru, State Grid acquired CDP RETI, the Legend Group acquired the mobile business of Motorola, DFM acquired

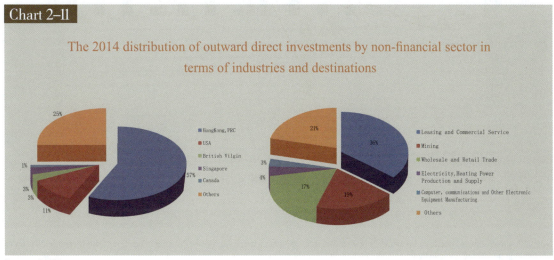

Chart 2–11

The 2014 distribution of outward direct investments by non-financial sector in terms of industries and destinations

Source: SAFE.

PSA Peugeot Citroen, and so forth. In particular, the acquisitions of the Noble Group and of Nidera by Cofco were the two largest two overseas agricultural investment projects.

(IV) Portfolio investments

Portfolio investments maintained a surplus. In 2014 net inflows of portfolio investments amounted to USD 82.4 billion, an increase of 56 percent year on year (see Chart 2–12). Since 2011 when the United States and the European countries were still suffering from the sovereign debt crisis, China's portfolio investment had recorded a net inflow for three consecutive years due to the growing inward portfolio investments. Different from the other economies with huge amounts of capital inflows and outflows, increased inward portfolio investments indicated that the Chinese capital market was becoming more attractive against the background of steady economic growth with an improved infrastructure and further opening.

Outward portfolio investments were developing rapidly on the basis of a small scale. In 2014 net outflows of outward portfolio investments amounted to USD 10.8 billion, twice the amount of net inflows in 2013. Along with the warming of overseas capital markets, especially

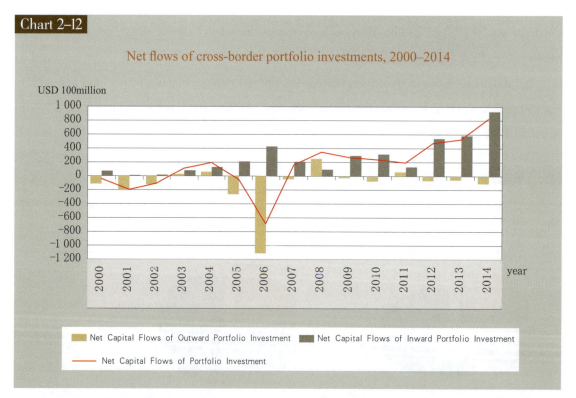

Notes: Positive outward portfolio investments refer to net inflows, otherwise net outflows. Positive inward portfolio investments refer to net inflows, otherwise net outflows.
Source: SAFE.

the USD bond market, domestic entities' enthusiasm about outward investment was rising. In terms of investment categories, the amount of outward equity security investments and the amount of bond investments stood at roughly the same scale, but the latter recorded a higher net outflow. Net outflows of bond investments totaled USD 9.4 billion, while net outflows of equity security investments totaled USD 1.4 billion. The preference for bond investments indicated a lower risk preference by domestic entities and increasing risk aversion. In terms of the investment entities, the banking sector increased its outward bond investments, with net outflows at USD 3.2 billion, an increase of 3.8 times over the net outflows in 2013. In addition, the net outflows of QDIIs totaled USD 9.6 billion, a 1.1 time increase over the outflows in 2013 and a historical high since the 2008 financial crisis.

Inward portfolio investment surged remarkably. In 2014 net inflows of inward portfolio investments amounted to USD 93.2 billion, up 60 percent year on year. In particular, portfolio equity investments recorded net inflows of USD 51.9 billion, and portfolio bond investments recorded net inflows of USD 41.3 billion, up by 59 percent and 61 percent respectively. There were three major sources of investment channels. The first source was QFIIs and RQFIIs whose investments grew rapidly due to the increased investment quota, and the total net inflows of QFIIs and RQFIIs amounted to USD 25.3 billion, up by 51 percent year on year. The second source was RMB investments in the domestic interbank bond market by foreign institutions, with the net inflows amounting to USD 32.9 billion. The third source was money raised from H-share by domestic institutions who issued stocks on the Hong Kong Market, totaling USD 34.2 billion and recording growth of 98 percent year on year.

(V) Other investments

Other investments changed from net inflows in the first half of the year to net outflows in the second half of the year. Other investments are an important factor influencing China's BOP status. In 2014 other investment inflows accounted for 77 percent of the capital and financial account inflows, and their outflows accounted for 88 percent of the capital and financial account outflows. Other investments frequently change between surpluses and deficits due to uncertainties both domestically and internationally, indicating rising volatility and procyclicality. In 2014 other investments recorded net outflows of USD 252.8 billion, whereas in 2013 they recorded net inflows of USD 72.2 billion. In particular, loans, net outflows of currency and deposits, and trade credits came USD 108.1 billion, USD 78.3 billion, and USD 70.8 billion respectively, and the other items recorded net inflows of USD 4.4 billion (see Chart 2–13).

Outward other investments grew significantly. In 2014 net outflows of outward other investments amounted to USD 303 billion, an increase of 1.1 times the net outflows in 2013. This was driven by the rising external assets in the banking sector. In particular, overseas currencies and deposits increased by USD 159.7 billion, whereas in 2013 it increased by only USD 7.4 billion. This represented a twentyfold increase year on year. External loans increased by USD 68.8 billion, up by 14 percent year on year. The rising outward other investment reflected the changing expectations of domestic entities regarding the exchange rate, interest rate, and market environment, driving them to increase their allocation of assets in the international market.

The liabilities of other investments increased with dropping rate. In 2014 inward other investments recorded net inflows (i.e., net increases of external liabilities) of USD 50.2 billion, down by 77 percent year on year. There were two main sources for this change. One was the increase in currencies and deposits, which totaled USD 81.4 billion, representing an increase of 7 percent year on year. The other was borrowed external loans, which changed from an increase of USD 93.4 billion to a decrease of USD 34.3 billion because domestic

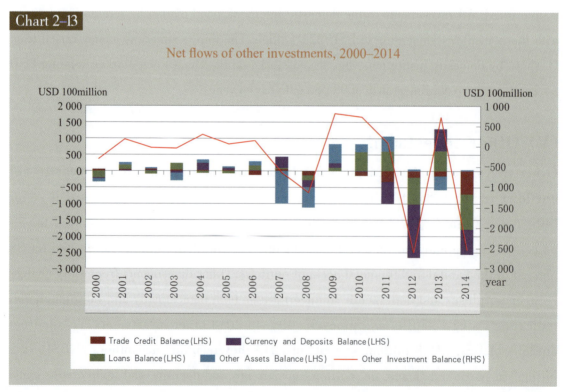

Chart 2–13

Net flows of other investments, 2000–2014

Source: SAFE.

banks reduced their external trade finance liabilities, such as letters of credit and payments by overseas banks to avoid risks.

Box 4

The practice of macro prudential regulation applied to foreign exchange administration of banks

Since the 2008 international financial crisis, international organizations and regulatory institutions have realized that micro prudential regulation alone may be insufficient to prevent against procyclicality and multi–sector risks. Thus, macro prudential regulation is gradually attracting more attention. In addition, in the process of the "Five Changes," that is, how to ease micro prudential regulation on enterprises and individuals, strengthen prudential regulation on banks with a comprehensive perspective over their foreign exchange inflows and outflows, and establish a gradually counter–cyclical regulatory mechanism to relieve and even eliminate the possible shocks of cross–border capital flow fluctuations are very important for the SAFE.

1. Two practices of macro prudential regulation of the banks' foreign exchange inflow and outflows

Regulation of the position on a cash basis carried out at the end of 2010 to the beginning of 2011. In the fourth quarter of 2010, RMB appreciation expectations were rising significantly, which led to rapid growth in the domestic banks' net foreign exchange sales on forward contract. To hedge their own foreign exchange position, banks sold their foreign exchange in spot markets (which led to a decreased position on a cash basis), thus the central bank's net foreign exchange purchases increased significantly. To deal with this, SAFE released two notices, in November 2010 and March 2011, applying lower limit on the banks' foreign exchange position on a cash basis and limiting the banks' open forward foreign exchange position to be sold in the spot market, thus driving the banks to adjust their quotations on forward foreign exchange sales and purchases and limiting their clients' forward position to deal with abnormal cross–border capital inflows. After announcement of these policies, the banks' forward open position with their clients no longer climbed and the central bank's pressures on foreign exchange purchases were relieved. In addition, the banks' capability to guard against risks was improved since they had increased their foreign exchange position. Moreover, pressures for foreign exchange purchases due to the turbulence in the foreign exchange market at the end of 2011 were calmed (see Chart C4–1). In April 2012, these temporary measures were cancelled due to the more balanced foreign exchange market and the less abnormal cross–border capital inflows. **Measures on the lower limit of overall foreign exchanges sales and purchases were launched in May 2015**. Since the end of 2012, the RMB picked up a trend of appreciation expectations and the surplus in the foreign exchange sales and purchases in the non– banking rose from a low level. The rebound accelerated in 2013, with the surplus in the first quarter totaling USD 169.3 billion with the main source from foreign exchange loans extended by domestic banks to enterprises to substitute for foreign exchange purchases. The SAFE adjusted the regulations on the banks' overall position and linked their overall position limit with their foreign exchange loans and deposits. Banks whose loan–to– deposit ratios (the ratio of outstanding domestic foreign exchange loans to outstanding foreign exchange deposits) exceeded the referential threshold would be asked to adjust their overall position to a level over their lower limit before s designated time. After their

Chart C4–1

The outstanding forward balance and the foreign exchange position on a cash basis, 2010–2012

Source: SAFE.

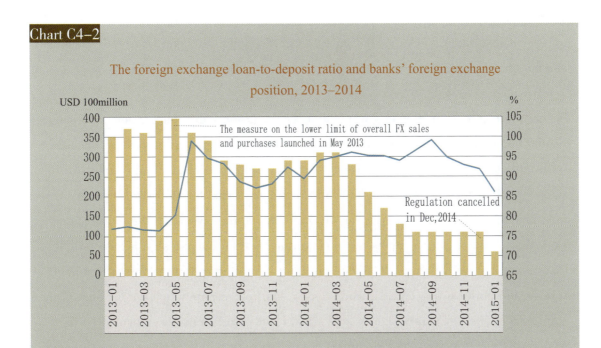

Chart C4–2

The foreign exchange loan-to-deposit ratio and banks' foreign exchange position, 2013–2014

Note: Policy banks are excluded.
Sources: PBC, SAFE.

release, on the one hand the banks increased their overall foreign position and on the other controlled and decreased their outstanding domestic foreign exchange loans. The outstanding domestic foreign exchange loans decreased month by month and the foreign exchange loan–to–deposit ratio was under control (see Chart C4–2). In December 2014, the SAFE eliminated the temporary measures with supply and demand adjustments in the foreign exchange market.

2. Outlook for the banking sector's foreign exchange macro prudential regulation

First of all, the scale of the banking sector's foreign exchange sales and purchases grew rapidly, which provided sufficient sources to allocate their funds in domestic and overseas markets as well as for the nonbanking sector's financial operations with a procyclical characteristic. The banks' behavior, including their external assets and liabilities allocations, financing from domestic and overseas markets, and foreign exchange derivatives transactions, resonated with the RMB appreciation expectation. The procyclicality also drove enterprises to conduct financial operations in both domestic and overseas markets and intensified the pressures of the foreign exchange market fluctuations and foreign reserve growth.

Second, foreign exchange macro prudential regulation on banks should focus on macro prudential adjustments with counter–cyclicality on cross–border foreign exchange transactions to guard against abnormal cross–border capital flows and to improve the status of the balance of payments. To realize this target, monitoring should be intensified from macro, medium, and micro levels so that a monitoring system of the banks' foreign exchange abnormal fluctuations will be established. To choose appropriate policies, discrimination should be made among ordinary regulatory policies, against temporary shocks and policies against material shocks. Market–oriented regulations should be employed against temporary shocks, and capital flow regulations accompanied by macro prudential measures should be employed against material shocks to ensure financial stability.

Third, macro prudential regulation of the banking sector's foreign exchange transactions should improve analysis of the targets of the regulation and the designation of the policy instruments. From the perspective of regulation, the banking sector's foreign exchange liabilities, foreign exchange assets, and off–balance sheet financing may be the target of regulation. In terms of instruments, the effects of the overall position of the banking sector's foreign exchange sales and purchases require further review. In addition, current measures, such as the banks' short–term external debt limits and the annual review of the banks' foreign exchange business compliance must be improved. Moreover, international experience should be taken into consideration to improve preparation of the instruments.

III.International Investment Position

Net external assets decreased. By the end of 2014 China's external assets[1] and liabilities totaled USD 6408.7 billion and USD 4 632.3 billion respectively, increasing by 7 percent and 16 percent year on year. The degree of financial opening (the ratio of gross external assets and liabilities to GDP) was 107 percent, 1.5 percentage points lower than that in 2013. Net external assets amounted to USD 1 776.4 billion, a decrease of USD 219.6 billion and its ratio to GDP was 17 percent, 3.9 percentage points lower than the ratio in 2013 (see Chart 3–1 and Chart 3–2). The decrease in net external assets [2] was driven by two factors. One was non-transactional factors, such as the exchange rate and price fluctuations, which led to significant valuation fluctuations of external assets, with reserve assets as the main component. The other was the revision of historical data by some reporting agencies, which led to increased external liabilities.

Changing external assets reflected the strategy of encouraging foreign exchange held by the private sector. By the end of 2014, outstanding international reserve assets totaled

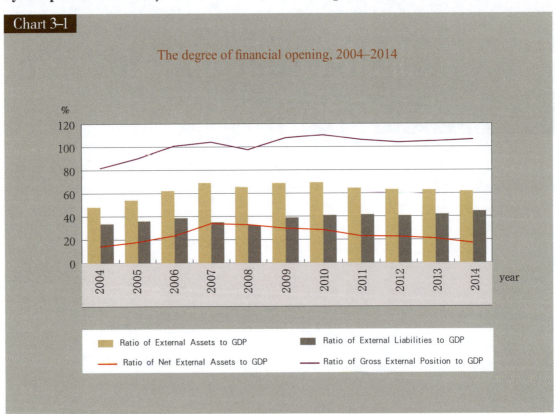

Chart 3–1

The degree of financial opening, 2004–2014

Sources: SAFE, NBS.

---

① External assets and liabilities include direct investments, portfolio investments and deposits, and loans. Outward direct investments are categorized as external financial assets because the shares held by domestic investors in overseas enterprises have the same nature as equity investments of portfolio investments, with the exception that their influence on the operations of the target enterprises may be different, and vice versa for inward direct investments.

② Net external assets do not equal the current account balance in the BOP. For detailed analysis, see *China's Balance-of-Payments Report* 2013, Box 3.

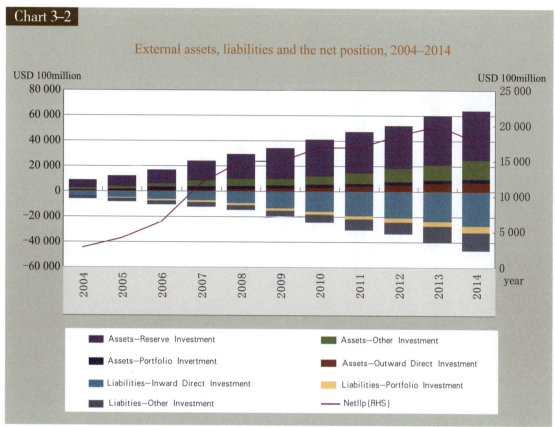

Chart 3–2

External assets, liabilities and the net position, 2004–2014

Source: SAFE.

USD 3 899.3 billion, which was still the largest component of the external assets and accounted for 61 percent of the total external assets, 4 percentage points lower than the ratio in 2013 and a historical low since 2004. The private sector accelerated its going–out investment. It preferred traditional investment due to its preference for low risks. Outward direct investments and other investments, such as loans and deposits, amounted to USD 2 246.9 billion, accounting for 35 percent of total external assets, which represented a historical high. Outward portfolio investment assets totaled USD 262.5 billion, accounting for 4 percent of total external assets, 0.2 percentage point lower than the ratio in 2013 (see Chart 3–3).

External liabilities in terms of outward portfolio investments grew rapidly. By the end of 2014, affected by multiple factors such as the trend of domestic enterprises listing in overseas market and the more open domestic capital market, external portfolio investment liabilities amounted to USD 514.3 billion, growth of 33 percent year on year. Its growth rate was higher than the growth rate of FDI liabilities and other investment liabilities, including loans and deposits, by about 20 percentage points. Portfolio investment liabilities accounted for 11 percent of total external liabilities, 1.4 percentage points higher than the ratio in

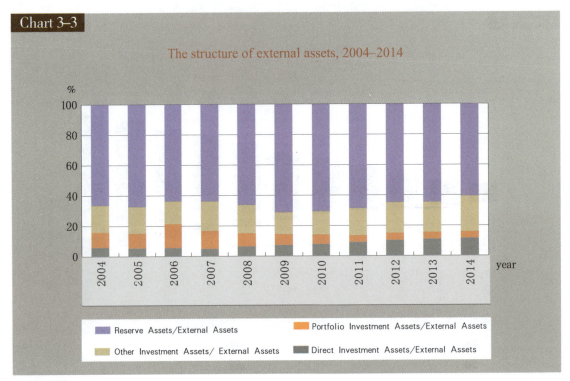

Chart 3–3

The structure of external assets, 2004–2014

Reserve Assets/External Assets
Portfolio Investment Assets/External Assets
Other Investment Assets/ External Assets
Direct Investment Assets/External Assets

Source: SAFE.

2013. FDI liabilities totaled USD 2 677.9 billion, an increase by 15 percent and continuing to be the most important source of external liabilities, accounting for 58 percent of the total external liabilities. Due to the impact of the exchange rate, the interest rate, and the RMB internationalization, as well as the revision of the historical data by some reporting agencies, other investment liabilities, including loans and liabilities, increased by 13 percent year on year and accounted for 31 percent of total external liabilities, a decrease by 0.8 percentage point compared with the ratio in 2013 (see Chart 3–4).

Net external liabilities of the private sector increased further. As an immature net creditor, China's net external assets concentrated on the public sector (including the central bank and the government), and the private sector (including banks and enterprises) became the major source of net external liabilities. Hence there was sectoral mismatch in terms of external assets and liabilities. By the end of 2014, China's net external liabilities totaled USD 2 122.9 billion, after excluding the reserve assets (USD 3 899.3 billion), increasing by 13 percent year on year and accounting for 20 percent of GDP, representing growth by 0.6 percentage point from the ratio in 2013 and by 10 percentage points from the ratio in 2008.

Chart 3-4

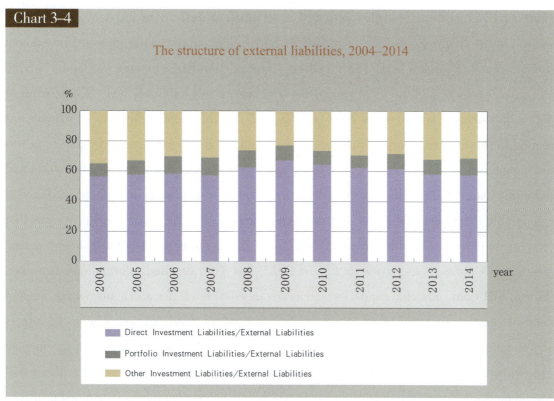

The structure of external liabilities, 2004–2014

Source: SAFE.

Chart 3-5

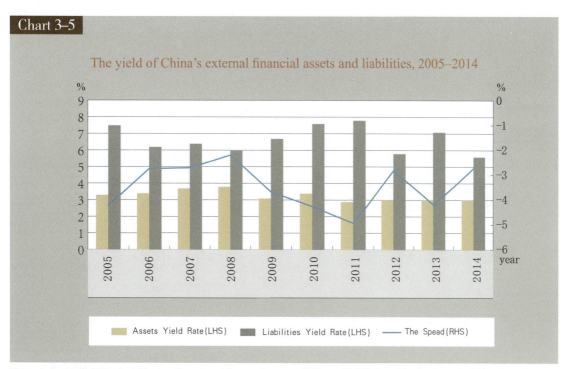

The yield of China's external financial assets and liabilities, 2005–2014

Notes: 1. Assets (liabilities) yield rate = [investment income (payments)]/[(asset (liability) position by the end of this year + the asset (liability) position by the end of the last year)/2].

2. The spread = the asset yield rate + the liabilities yield rate.

Source: SAFE.

Outward investment income recorded a structural deficit. In 2014, the investment income of the BOP recorded a deficit of USD 59.9 billion. In particular, outward investment income receipts totaled USD 183.1 billion, external liabilities income payments totaled USD 242.9 billion, and the yield spread between assets and liabilities was −2.7 percentage points, the smallest spread since 2009 (see Chart 3–5). The negative investment income was related to the holders of China's external assets and liabilities who decided that China was not compatible with economies with a high market orientation and with external assets and liabilities mainly held by the private sector. In fact, China's outward investment income was comparable to international levels. But the major component of the external liabilities was FDI (60 percent of the total), with a relatively high yield, leading to negative net investment income (see *China's Balance–of–Payments Report 2012*, Box 1 for detailed information). However, through FDI China attracted capital as well as advanced technologies and management, created domestic employment and taxes, and developed and international market. The social effects and economic income were far more than the fiscal costs. In addition, a part of the income expenditures on foreign shareholders was reinvested tin domestic enterprises without real capital outflows. After excluding reinvestments, China's investment income remained positive.

Table 3-1 China's IIP by the end of 2014[1]

Unit: USD 100 million

Items	Ranking	At the end of 2014
Net IIP [2]	1	17 764
A. Assets	2	64 087
1.Outward direct investments	3	7 443
2.Porfolio investments	4	2 625
2.1 Equity securities	5	1 613
2.2 Debt securities	6	1 012
3. Other investments	7	15 026
3.1 Trade credits	8	4 677
3.2 Loans	9	3 747
3.3 Currency and deposits	10	5 541
3.4 Other assets	11	1 061
4. Reserve investments	12	38 993
4.1 Monetary gold	13	401
4.2 Special drawing rights	14	105
4.3 Reserve position in the fund	15	57
4.4 Foreign exchange	16	38 430
B. Liabilities	17	46 323
1. Inward foreign direct investments	18	26 779
2. Portfolio investments	19	5 143
2.1 Equity securities	20	3 693
2.2 Debt securities	21	1 449
3. Other investments	22	14 402
3.1 Trade credits	23	3 344
3.2 Loans	24	5 720
3.3 Currency and deposits	25	5 030
3.4 Other liabilities	26	308

Source:SAFE.

---

[1] In line with BOP statistical principles, International Investment Position statistics records external positions between residents and nonresidents, no matter the positions are in domestic currency or in foreign currencies.

[2] Net IIP = asset−liability. A positive position means net assets and a negative position means net liabilities. The data are calculated using rounded−off figures.

IV. Operation of the Foreign Exchange Market and the RMB Exchange Rate

(I) Trends in the RMB Exchange Rate

The RMB exchange rate against the USD declined slightly. At the end of 2014, the mid-price of the RMB exchange rate against the USD was 6.1190, down 0.4 percent from the end of 2013 (see Chart 4–1). Though the spot exchange rate of the interbank foreign exchange market (CNY) and the offshore market (CNH) declined by 2.4 percent and 2.6 percent respectively, globally the RMB still ranked as a stable currency (see Chart 4–2).

The multilateral RMB exchange rate appreciated against the currency market. According to the BIS, in 2014 the RMB nominal effective exchange rate appreciated by 6.41 percent. Deducting for the inflation, the real effective exchange rate appreciated by 6.39 percent (see Chart 4–3). In 2014, the extent of appreciation of the RMB nominal and real effective exchange rate ranked the 5th and 8th respectively among the 61 currencies observed by the BIS. Since the exchange rate regime reform in 2005, the RMB nominal and real effective exchange rate appreciated by 40.5 percent and 51.3 percent respectively, which ranked the 1st and 2nd respectively among the 61 currencies observed by the BIS.

The RMB exchange rate floated in two directions and its elasticity improved. From the perspective of the spot exchange rate (CNY, see Chart 4–4), from the beginning of 2014 to the middle of February, the spot trading price remained stable and generally stayed close

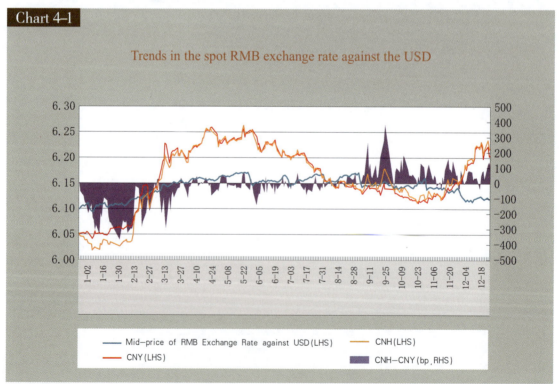

Chart 4–1

Trends in the spot RMB exchange rate against the USD

Mid-price of RMB Exchange Rate against USD (LHS)   CNH (LHS)

CNY (LHS)   CNH–CNY (bp, RHS)

Sources: CFETS, Reuters.

Chart 4–2

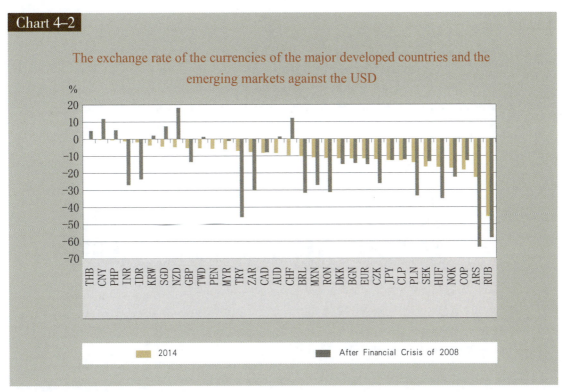

The exchange rate of the currencies of the major developed countries and the emerging markets against the USD

2014

After Financial Crisis of 2008

Sources: CFETS, Bloomberg.

Chart 4–3

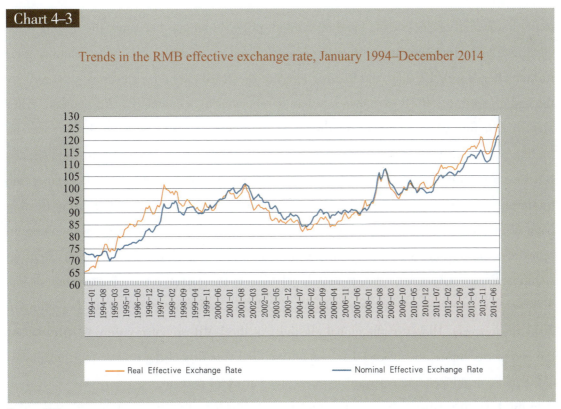

Trends in the RMB effective exchange rate, January 1994–December 2014

Real Effective Exchange Rate

Nominal Effective Exchange Rate

Sources: BIS.

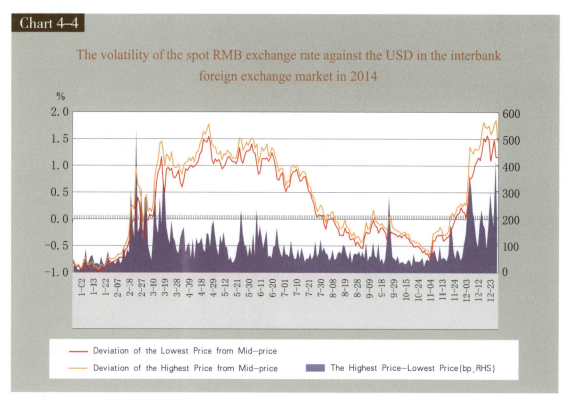

Chart 4-4

The volatility of the spot RMB exchange rate against the USD in the interbank foreign exchange market in 2014

Legend:
— Deviation of the Lowest Price from Mid–price
— Deviation of the Highest Price from Mid–price
▪ The Highest Price—Lowest Price (bp, RHS)

Sources: CFETS.

to the lower limit of the floating band of the mid–price. From late February, the trading price continued to decline and entered the depreciation band of the mid– price. The volatility grew further after March 17 when the floating band of the RMB exchange rate was enlarged. By the end of April, the RMB exchange rate had depreciated by a cumulative 2.8 percent. After May, the trading price no longer declined and gradually began to rebound. In August, the trading price returned to the appreciation band of the mid– price. From May to October, the RMB exchange rate appreciated by a cumulative 2.4 percent. In November and December, the trading price again weakened and gradually became closer to the upper limit of the floating band of the mid–price, with an cumulative depreciation of 1.5 percent in the two months. In terms of volatility, the implied volatility of the domestic and offshore option markets went up significantly (see Chart 4–5). The 6–month volatility of the domestic and offshore market was 2.78 percent and 3.47 percent respectively, up 87.2 and 86.8 percent from the beginning of 2014 respectively. However, the global elasticity of the RMB exchange rate was still low. At the end of December, the averaged six–month implied volatility of the twenty–four currencies of the major developed and emerging markets stood at 11.94 percent.

The interest rate spread between domestic and foreign currencies enlarged and led a

Chart 4–5

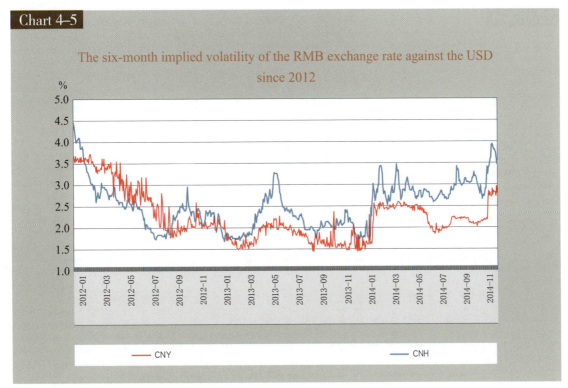

The six-month implied volatility of the RMB exchange rate against the USD since 2012

Note: The implied volatility of the flat option.
Source: Bloomberg.

larger USD premium in the foreign exchange forward market. In 2014 the exchange rates and interest rates had a further strengthened connection in the adjustment of their market mechanism. At the beginning of 2014, a large volume of net forward settlements by enterprises brought down the USD premium. Thereafter, as the RMB exchange rate depreciated, the demand for forward settlements was reduced and the demand for forwards purchases increased. As a result, the USD premium went up. Meanwhile, an increase in foreign currency deposits led to loose USD liquidity in the domestic market. However, RMB liquidity was generally tight, which resulted in a gradually larger interest rate spread between the domestic and foreign currencies, with the interest rate parity mechanism resulting in a larger USD premium (see Charts 4–6 and Charts4–7). At the end of 2014, the USD premium against the RMB in the one–year domestic delivered forward market, the offshore delivered forward market, and the offshore non–delivered forward market was 1 585bps, 1 550 bps, and 2 295 bps respectively, up by 1 135 bps, 1 090 bps, and 2 034 bps from the end of 2013 respectively.

The spread between the domestic and offshore RMB exchange rates narrowed substantially. At the beginning of 2014, the CNH was strong against the CNY and the spread was large. Thereafter, the CNH fluctuated up and down against the CNY and the spread began

Chart 4–6

The premium and discount of the one-year RMB forward rate against the USD in the domestic and offshore markets since 2013

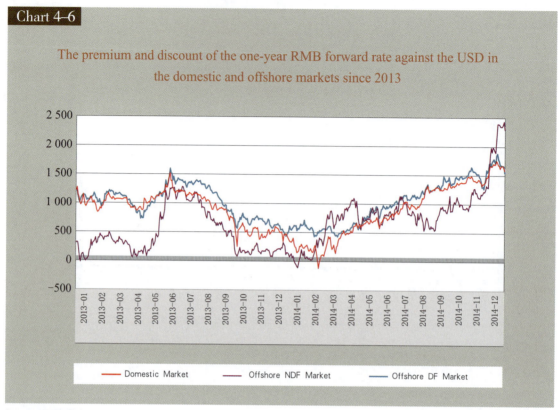

Sources: CFETS, Reuters.

Chart 4–7

The six-month interest rate spread between the RMB and the USD in the domestic market since 2013

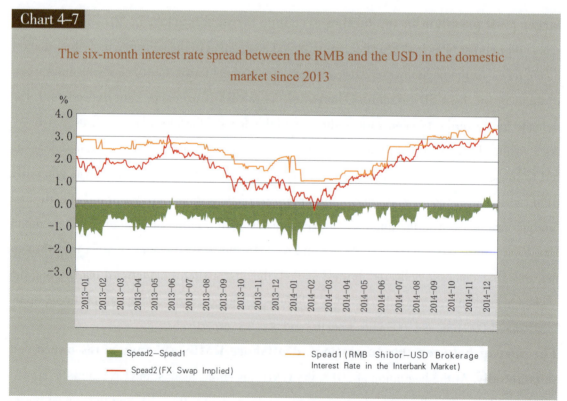

Sources: CFETS, Reuters.

to shrink (see Chart 4–8). The average daily spread between the CNH and the CNY stood at 79 bps in 2014, lower than the 83bps in 2013. As the RMB is not yet fully convertible, due to the differences in supply and demand relations and trading entities and regulatory policies, a spread between the domestic and offshore RMB exchange rate is a matter of necessity. As cross–border RMB business develops, market entities can flexibly choose their settlement currencies for cross–border transactions and trading places for foreign exchange purchases and sales. As a result, domestic and offshore RMB exchange rates will more influence on each other and their spread will shrink.

(II) Transactions in the Foreign Exchange Market

In 2014 the domestic RMB foreign exchange market saw a total trading volume of USD12.67 trillion (excluding foreign currency pairs), up 13.4 percent from 2013. The growth rate fell by 9.1 percent from 2013, which reflected a slowdown in cross–border trade and investment in the real economy and the substitute effect of the offshore RMB market to the domestic market. The daily average trading volume stood at USD 52.1 billion. The client and interbank

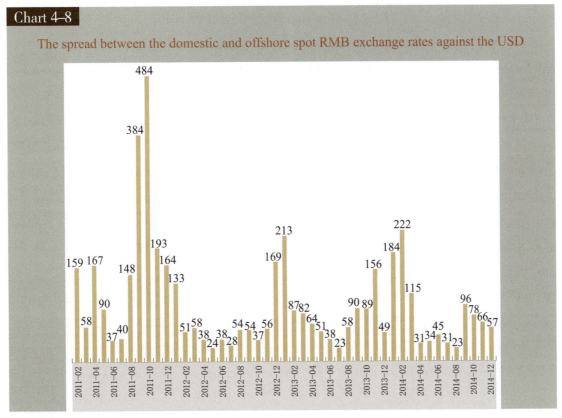

Chart 4–8

The spread between the domestic and offshore spot RMB exchange rates against the USD

Note: The absoute value of the average daily spread.
Sources: CFETS, Reuters.

Chart 4–9

Trading volume in China's foreign exchange market, 2002–2014

USD 100million

- Spot Market
- Derivatives Market

Sources: SAFE, CFETS.

foreign exchange markets saw a trading volume of USD 3.95 trillion and USD 8.81 trillion respectively.① The spot and derivatives markets saw a trading volume of 7.25 trillion and 5.51 trillion respectively (see Table 4–1 and Chart 4–9). Derivatives accounted for 43.2 percent of the total trading volume in the foreign exchange market, representing a historical high.

A slight increase in spot foreign exchange transactions. In 2014, the spot foreign exchange market saw a trading volume of USD 7.25 trillion, up 2.3 percent from 2013. Spot purchases and sales of foreign exchange in the client market totaled USD 3.13 trillion (including the banks themselves, but excluding the implementation of forwards), up 3.8 percent from 2013. The spot interbank foreign exchange market saw a trading volume of USD 4.12 trillion, up 1.2 percent from 2013. The share of USD transactions in the interbank market was 94.5 percent.

A small decrease in foreign exchange forward transactions. In 2014 the forward market saw a trading volume of USD 597.9 billion, down 1.1 percent from 2013. In the client market, forward purchases and sales of foreign exchange totaled USD 545 billion, down 4.7 percent from 2013. Forward purchases totaled USD 300.5 billion and forward sales totaled USD 244.4

① In the client market, the trading volume is the total amount of both the foreign exchange purchases and the foreign exchange sales. In the interbank market, the trading volume is unilateral transactions. The same as below.

billion, down 14.7 percent and up 11.1 percent from 2013 respectively (see Chart 4–10). Short–term transactions of less than 6 months accounted for about 63.4 percent of the total transactions (see Chart 4–11). In the interbank market, foreign exchange forwards totaled USD 52.9 billion, up 63.5 percent from 2013. In the client market, the trading volume of forward transactions fell. On the one hand, this reflected the substitute effects of options. The ratio of the volume of options trading to the volume of forwards trading increased from 9.0 percent in 2013 to 11.6 percent in 2014. On the other hand, it highlighted the weak awareness of market risks among some enterprises, which led to the rise in a cautious attitude involving the derivatives market.

A large increase in foreign exchange and currency swap transactions. In 2014 the cumulative foreign exchange and currency swap transactions totaled USD4.72 trillion, up 35.4 percent from 2013. The cumulative foreign exchange and currency swap transactions in the client market reached USD217.3 billion, up 1.7 times from 2013. Spot purchases/forward sales and spot sales/forward purchases stood at USD 19.2 billion and USD 198.1 billion respectively, up 36.3 percent and 1.9 times respectively. The cumulative foreign exchange and currency swap transactions in the interbank market reached USD 4.50 trillion, up 32.3 percent from 2013. The continuous activity in the swap market reflected closer connections between the foreign exchange market and the monetary market of domestic and foreign currencies and a

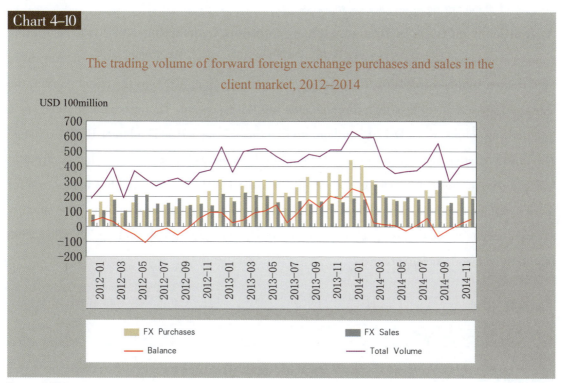

Chart 4–10

The trading volume of forward foreign exchange purchases and sales in the client market, 2012–2014

USD 100million

Source: SAFE.

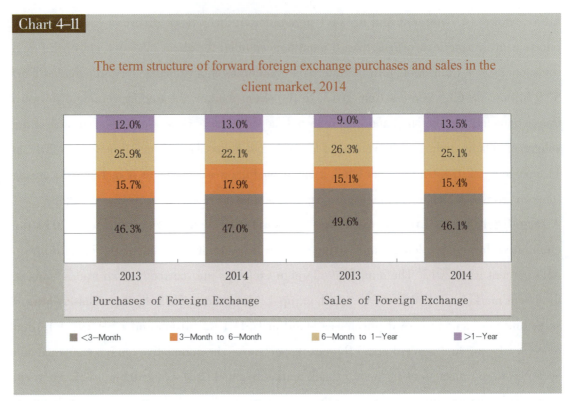

Chart 4–11

The term structure of forward foreign exchange purchases and sales in the client market, 2014

Source: SAFE.

new trend of managing assets across markets.

A significant increase in foreign exchange options transactions. In 2014 the trading volume of options totaled USD 192.8 billion, up 1.6 times from 2013. The client market saw a total trading volume of USD 62.9 billion, up 22.3 percent from 2013. In the client market, the share of transactions of less than three months was 41.3 percent. The interbank market saw a total trading volume of USD 129.9 billion, up five times from 2013. The larger RMB exchange rate elasticity after the reform can be attributed to the increase in options. Another contributor was the developing measures for options since August 2014. These enabled banks to offer more diversified options, such as call options, put options, and options portfolios. The monthly average trading volume of options from August to December of 2014 went up 3.3 times from that in the previous seven months.

Table 4-1 Transactions in the RMB/foreign exchange market, 2014   (100 million)

Products	Trading Volume
Spot	72 486
Client Market	31 255

(Continued)

Products	Trading Volume
Interbank Foreign Exchange Market	41 232
Forward	5 979
Client Market	5 450
Less than 3 months (including 3 months)	2 540
3 months to 1 year (including 1 year)	2 190
More than 1 year	720
Interbank Foreign Exchange Market	529
Less than 3 months (including 3 months)	392
3 months to 1 year (including 1 year)	132
More than 1 year	5
Foreign Exchange and Currency Swaps	47 168
Client Market	2 173
Interbank Foreign Exchange Market	44 995
Less than 3 months (including 3 months)	39 416
3 months to 1 year (including 1 year)	5 424
More than 1 year	154
Options	1 928
Client Market	629
Foreign Exchange Call Options/RMB Put Options	333
Foreign Exchange Put Options/RMB Call Options	297
Less than 3 months (including 3 months)	260
3 months to 1 year (including 1 year)	262
More than 1 year	108
Interbank Foreign Exchange Market	1 299
Foreign Exchange Call Options/RMB Put Options	653
Foreign Exchange Put Options/RMB Call Options	646
Less than 3 months (including 3 months)	1 060
3 months to 1 year (including 1 year)	238
More than 1 year	1
Total	127 561
Client Market	39 507
Interbank Foreign Exchange Market	88 054
Including: Spots	72 486
Forwards	5 979
Foreign Exchange and Currency Swaps	47 168
Options	1 928

Note: The trading volumes used here are all unilateral transactions and the data employ rounded-off numbers.
Sources: SAFE, CFETS.

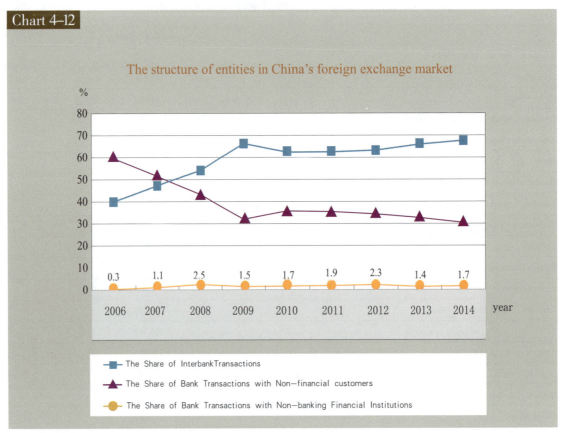

Chart 4–12

The structure of entities in China's foreign exchange market

- The Share of InterbankTransactions
- The Share of Bank Transactions with Non–financial customers
- The Share of Bank Transactions with Non–banking Financial Institutions

Sources: SAFE, CFETS.

The structure of market entities was basically stable. Proprietary trading by banks continued to dominate the market (see Chart 4–12). In 2014 interbank transactions accounted for 67.7 percent of total transactions in the foreign exchange market; in 2013 the figure was 66 percent. The share of non–financial institutions fell to 30.5 percent; in 2013 the figure was 32.7 percent. The share of non–banking financial institutions increased to 1.7 percent, higher than the 0.3 percent in 2013. Non–banking financial institutions were still a weak part of the market entities in the domestic foreign exchange market.

A drop in interbank foreign currency trading. In 2014 nine currency pairs saw a total trading volume of USD 60.6 billion, down 5.7 percent from 2013. As the largest trading category, spot transactions saw a trading volume of USD 44.9 billion, up 29.8 percent from 2013. The Euro/USD currency pair still had the largest trading volume (see Chart 4–13). The USD/HKD and AUD/USD pairs ranked 2nd and 3rd. The three currency pairs cumulatively accounted for 85.9 percent of the total trading volume.

Chart 4–13

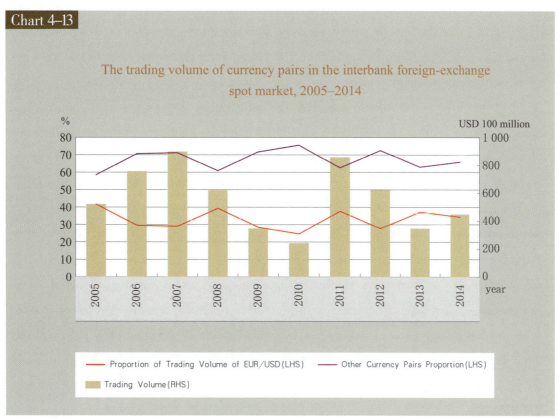

The trading volume of currency pairs in the interbank foreign-exchange spot market, 2005–2014

Source: CFETS.

Box 5

A brief analysis of the hedging costs of current foreign exchange derivatives

In 2014 the volatility of the RMB exchange rate increased. Nevertheless, rather than increase, the foreign exchange derivative transactions declined. From April to December, the monthly average signed contracts for forward purchases and sales of foreign exchange was reduced by 33.4 percent from that in the first quarter of 2014 and by 15.4 percent from that in 2013. Some believe that the hedging costs were high because the forward rate had a strong USD premium, thus affecting the motivation for hedging by enterprises. However, this explanation involves a misunderstanding.

The hedging costs can be interpreted as transaction costs and holding costs. The transaction cost is the spread between the purchasing price and the selling price. The larger the spread, the higher the cost or the lower the profit an investor can make during the purchase or sale of a financial product. An option is one kind of financial product that requires that the fees be paid separately. Therefore, the option fee is also part of the transaction cost. The holding cost is the collateral or credit an investor has to add after he gains a financial product to compensate for the loss in market value due to volatility in the price. If the price is too volatile such that the collateral or the credit is used up and the investor cannot continue to hold the financial product, the holding cost or the revaluation loss will become a real loss. It is normal for hedging to have both transaction and holding costs. A mature and sound hedging strategy should choose suitable derivatives to control the risks instead of purchasing risks in line with its own risk exposure and tolerance.

Some enterprises understand the hedging costs from a lopsided view, such as the "price-quality ratio". Unlike the mature markets, gaining profits is a main reason for some enterprises to carry out derivative transactions, which is a practical financial view. For example, when some enterprises decide whether to choose forward purchases or spot sales for their future export income, a major consideration is based on their judgment on the comparison between forward rates and the trend in the foreign exchange rate. It is not

Chart C5-1

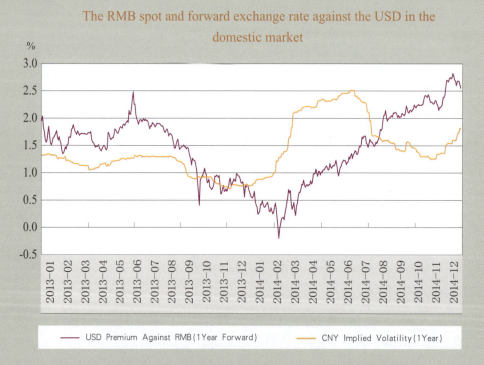

The RMB spot and forward exchange rate against the USD in the domestic market

——— USD Premium Against RMB (1 Year Forward)   ——— CNY Implied Volatility (1 Year)

Note: 1. The spot exchange rate is the closing inquiry price in the interbank foreign exchange spot market.
2. The USD forward premium rate = the bps of the USD premium in the interbank forward market/spot exchange rate.
Source: CFETS.

their priority to control the risks. If the forward rate is not expected to be higher than the foreign exchange rate in the future, which means they cannot save money or gain money, they do not hedge. During the past few years, this understanding has been impacted by the market environment. The RMB forward rate reflected the positive interest spread between domestic and foreign currencies and maintained a depreciation. Meanwhile, the spot exchange rate had a lower volatility and showed a unilateral appreciation. Under such circumstances, enterprises could always make money by forward purchases (unlike forward sales). Those experiences led some enterprises to misunderstand that hedging is necessary to earn money and to ignore its basic function to deal with the volatility in foreign exchange risks.

As the RMB exchange rate has reached at a balanced level and dual fluctuations have become a new normal, enterprises should adjust their old trading habits that focused on judging or betting on the appreciation or depreciation trend of the RMB exchange rate. Enterprises should establish strict financial discipline for hedging in order to manage their foreign exchange risks and should not let market judgments substitute for market operations.

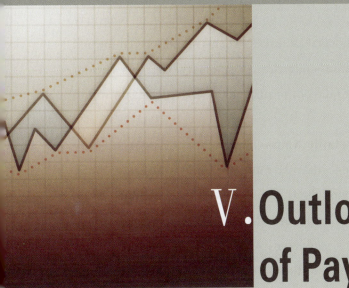

V.Outlook for the Balance of Payments

In 2015 China's balance of payments will maintain its new normal, with a surplus in the current account and the capital and financial account fluctuating in two directions.

The current account will remain in surplus. On the one hand, the recovery in the global economy, especially the recovery in the U.S. economy, will stabilize external demand for Chinese exports. Meanwhile, low international commodity prices and steady domestic demand may further depress import prices and demand. As a result, China's net exports may continue to grow. On the other hand, the deficit in trade in services and investment income may still be high due to Chinese residents' high overseas travel expenses and foreign-owned companies' high profit remittances to their parent countries. In summary, China's current account will remain in surplus in 2015, and the ratio of the surplus to GDP will remain within the reasonable range of international standards.

Cross-border capital flows may be more volatile. Cross-border capital flows can easily be affected by changes in the exchange rates, interest rates, and market expectations. Internationally, the U.S. economy is recovering, and the U.S. Fed may start to raise rates in the second half of 2015. Meanwhile, turbulence such as the unsettled European debt negotiations and the outbreak of geographic political conflicts may intensify international financial market fluctuations, which will induce international capital to flow to the United States and to strong currencies such as the USD and will impose capital outflow pressures on the emerging market economies. Domestically, during domestic economic transitions from a slowdown in economic growth, difficult structural adjustments and absorption of the effects of the previous economic stimulus policies to the new normal, market participants will be sensitive to slowdowns in economic growth and to the accumulation of risks in the financial and real estate industries. They may continue to adjust their balance-sheet structure by accumulating foreign-currency assets and deleveraging foreign-currency liabilities. As a result, China's capital and financial account may experience more volatile fluctuations in two directions.

Although international and domestic unsteadiness and uncertainties will bring more volatility to China's cross-border capital flows, China's BOP balance is expected to remain within an appropriate and controllable range. First, the Chinese economy is expected to grow at approximately 7 percent, which may be lower than earlier but it is still a medium-to-high growth rate. As the reforms are releasing dividends, the Chinese economy will continue to develop and thus will support the stable performance of the RMB exchange rate and the BOP situation. Second, the surplus in trade in goods and direct investments is still the major source of the BOP surplus. As China's exports are upgraded from labor-intensive products to technical–intensive products, some major equipment–manufacturing industries, such as the high–speed train industry, will become a new highlight in China's exports. This also indicates that China still has comparative advantages in terms of exports. Meanwhile, as the world's largest consumption market and with the implementation of the reforms and the opening–up of the domestic financial markets, China will continue to invite foreign capital flows, especially long–term foreign capital inflows. Finally, with adequate foreign exchange reserves, China is sufficiently strong to withstand external shocks. Meanwhile, as the Chinese economy becomes more open, cross–border capital can flow more conveniently and through more channels, which will require close monitoring of arbitrage cross–border capital flows in certain fields.

Box 6

The theory and practice of the combination of macroeconomic policy adjustments in the emerging market economies

In the 1950s, after studying the international economic situation during the period, the Canadian economist Mundell proposed the famous Impossible Trinity Theory. According to this theory, it is impossible to simultaneously have all three of the following–an independent monetary policy, free capital flows, and a stable exchange rate. The maximum is to pursue two policies simultaneously at the expense of the third. However, the Impossible Trinity Theory is a highly abstract theory, which considers only the extremes in policy combinations. The complex macroeconomic environment actually has created middle path based on this theory. During the recent financial crisis, although many economies, especially the emerging market economies, introduced different types of stimulus measures regarding monetary and fiscal policies, capital account management, and exchange rate regulations, those measures were basically under the guidance of the Impossible Trinity Theory.

Throughout the crisis, the Brazilian government and its central bank stuck to their independent monetary policy and actively adjusted domestic interest rates to keep inflation within a reasonable range. Meanwhile, the authorities switched between foreign exchange intervention and capital controls to identify the dynamic equilibrium between a stable exchange rate and free flows of capital. At the early stage of the crisis when the domestic currency faced pressures of appreciation, the Brazilian authorities implemented financial and capital taxation, a capital control tool, to stabilize the exchange rate. After the exchange rate was relatively stable, the authorities progressively lifted the capital controls and increased their tolerance for exchange rate fluctuations.

Chart C6–1

Adjustments in the Brazilian policy combinations

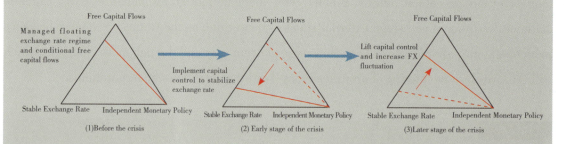

Before and after the crisis, the core of the Mexican policy combinations was to allow a free flow of capital. When the exchange rate fluctuated dramatically, the Mexican central bank implemented policies such as foreign exchange option auctions and direct interventions in the exchange rate. To obtain exchange rate stability, the Mexican authorities intervened in the foreign exchange market at the expense of monetary policy independence. After the exchange rate was stable, the Mexican authorities ended their intervention and restored the independent monetary policy. In our view, the policy combination of the Mexican government and the central bank was to continuously look for a relative equilibrium between an independent monetary policy and a stable exchange rate.

Chart C6–2

The Mexican policy adjustment combinations

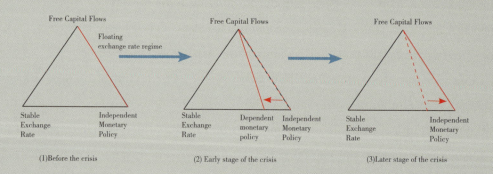

From the perspective of policy combinations, Russia was dedicated to stripping monetary policy from the framework of foreign exchange controls before the crisis. The purpose was to achieve an independent monetary policy. With the outbreak of the crisis, Russia learned from the previous ruble crisis and actively regulated the foreign exchange market, i.e., to ensure a stable exchange rate at the expense of an independent monetary policy. As the situation improved, Russia returned to the track of maintaining an independent monetary policy. Under the framework of the Impossible Trinity Theory, Russia's equilibrium always focuses on free flows of capital and adjusts dynamically between a fixed exchange rate regime and an independent monetary policy.

Chart C6-3

The Russian policy adjustment combinations

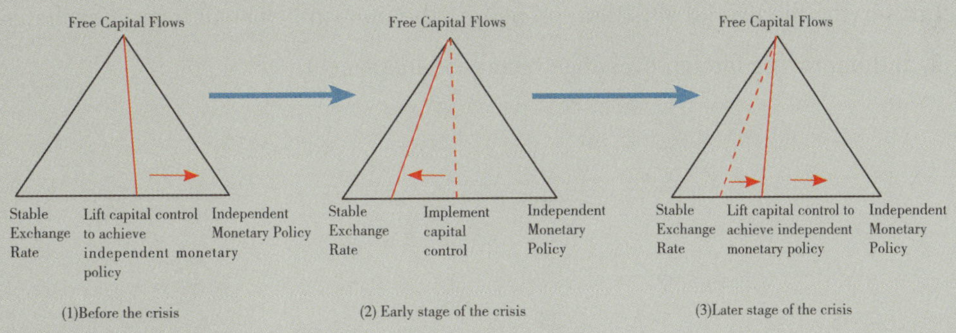

Free Capital Flows	Free Capital Flows	Free Capital Flows
Stable Exchange Rate / Lift capital control to achieve independent monetary policy / Independent Monetary Policy	Stable Exchange Rate / Implement capital control / Independent Monetary Policy	Stable Exchange Rate / Lift capital control to achieve independent monetary policy / Independent Monetary Policy
(1)Before the crisis	(2) Early stage of the crisis	(3)Later stage of the crisis

The above analysis demonstrates that the emerging market economies mainly used exchange rate tools to deal with the crisis, while the advanced economies chose to push down the interest rate curves in order to stimulate the economy. Meanwhile, in the long run, the key to the policy combinations in the emerging market economies is always an independent monetary policy, i.e., to maintain stable domestic prices. As one of the emerging market economies, China is also facing the impossible trinity issue. To ensure an independent monetary policy, China will act according to the targets of the Third Plenary Session of CPC's 18th Central Committee, further improve the RMB exchange rate formation mechanism, and adapt to the two-way opening up of the capital market and the higher degree of cross-border capital and financial convertibility.

In 2015, in the face of the complex international and domestic situations, the foreign exchange administration will more actively promote reforms and innovations to adapt to the new normal in the balance of payments and foreign exchange situations. To achieve a general equilibrium in the balance of payments and to guard against the shocks of cross–border capital flows, the foreign exchange administration will follow the requirements of the five transformations and push forward the key reforms in the convertibility of the RMB capital account. The major measures will include: first, deepening the reforms by accelerating the convertibility of the RMB capital account and actively pushing forward development of the foreign exchange market; Second, acting in accordance with the legislative requirements, simplifying administration, delegating power, and further facilitating trade and services; Third, transforming administration, accelerating the construction of macro–prudential–related external debts and capital flow management, and improving policy reserves and response plans; Fourth, firmly cracking down on illegal foreign exchange operations and criminal activities, and placing high pressure on abnormal cross–border capital flows; and fifth, adhering to the target of serving the overall situation, promoting the innovative use of foreign exchange reserve assets, and improving foreign exchange reserve management.

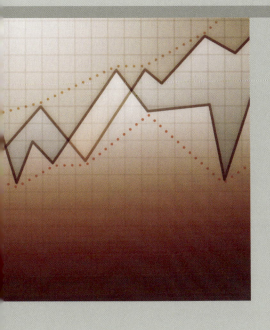

2014 中国国际收支报告
China's Balance of Payments Report

附　录　统计资料
Appendix　Statistics

一、国际收支[①]

I. Balance of Payments

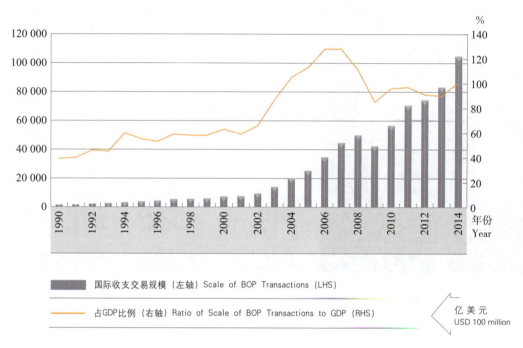

中国国际收支交易规模及其占 GDP 比例
China's Scale of BOP Transactions and Its Ratio to GDP

国际收支交易规模（左轴）Scale of BOP Transactions (LHS)

占GDP比例（右轴）Ratio of Scale of BOP Transactions to GDP (RHS)

亿美元
USD 100 million

① 资料来源：国家外汇管理局；IMF《国际收支统计》、《国际金融统计》；环亚经济数据库。
Sources: State Administration of Foreign Exchange; IMF, Balance of Payments Statistics, International Financial.

中国经常项目差额与资本和金融项目差额

China's Current Account Balance & Capital and Financial Account Balance

■ 经常项目差额 Current Account Balance

■ 资本和金融项目差额 Capital and Financial Account Balance

亿美元
USD 100 million

中国国际收支概览表（1）

China's Balance of Payments Abridged（1）

项目 Item	年份 Year	1982	1983	1984	1985	1986	1987	1988
一、经常账户差额 Current Account Balance		**57**	**42**	**20**	**−114**	**−70**	**3**	**−38**
贷方 Credit		254	254	293	301	312	405	479
借方 Debit		197	211	273	415	382	402	518
A.货物和服务差额 Goods and Services Balance		**48**	**26**	**1**	**−125**	**−74**	**3**	**−41**
贷方 Credit		237	233	268	283	298	392	459
借方 Debit		189	207	267	408	372	389	500
a.货物差额 Goods Balance		42	20	0	−131	−91	−17	−53
贷方 Credit		211	207	239	251	258	347	411
借方 Debit		169	187	239	382	349	364	464
b.服务差额 Services Balance		6	6	0	6	18	20	13
贷方 Credit		26	26	29	31	40	44	49
借方 Debit		20	20	29	25	23	25	36
B.收益差额 Income Balance		**4**	**12**	**15**	**8**	**−0**	**−2**	**−2**
贷方 Credit		10	15	19	14	9	10	15
借方 Debit		6	3	4	5	9	12	16
C.经常转移差额 Current Transfers Balance		5	5	4	2	4	2	4
贷方 Credit		7	6	6	4	5	4	6
借方 Debit		2	1	2	2	1	2	1
二、资本和金融项目差额 Capital and Financial Account Balance		**−17**	**−14**	**−38**	**85**	**65**	**27**	**53**
贷方 Credit		36	30	45	212	213	192	203
借方 Debit		53	44	83	127	148	164	150
A.资本账户差额 Capital Account Balance		**0**	**0**	**0**	**0**	**0**	**0**	**0**
贷方 Credit		0	0	0	0	0	0	0
借方 Debit		0	0	0	0	0	0	0
B.金融账户差额 Financial Account Balance		**−17**	**−14**	**−38**	**85**	**65**	**27**	**53**

单位：亿美元
Unit: USD 100 million

项目 Item	年份 Year	1982	1983	1984	1985	1986	1987	1988
贷方 Credit		36	30	45	212	213	192	203
借方 Debit		53	44	83	127	148	164	150
1.直接投资差额 Direct Investment Balance		4	8	13	13	18	17	23
贷方 Credit		4	9	14	20	22	23	32
借方 Debit		0	1	1	6	5	6	9
2.证券投资差额 Portfolio Investment Balance		0	−6	−16	30	16	11	9
贷方 Credit		0	2	9	30	16	12	12
借方 Debit		0	8	26	0	0	1	3
3.其他投资差额 Other Investment Balance		−21	−16	−34	41	32	0	20
贷方 Credit		31	20	22	162	175	157	159
借方 Debit		52	35	56	120	143	157	138
三、储备资产变动额 Reserve Assets		**−42**	**−27**	**5**	**54**	**17**	**−17**	**−5**
贷方 Credit		1	0	7	56	19	0	1
借方 Debit		43	27	2	2	1	17	5
其中：外汇储备差额 Foreign Exchange Reserves		**−43**	**−19**	**7**	**56**	**12**	**−15**	**−4**
四、净误差与遗漏 Net Errorsand Omissions		**3**	**−2**	**12**	**−25**	**−12**	**−14**	**−10**

Statistics; CEIC Database.

中国国际收支概览表（2）

China's Balance of Payments Abridged(2)

项目 Item	年份 Year	1989	1990	1991	1992	1993	1994	1995
一、经常账户差额 **Current Account Balance**		**−43**	**120**	**133**	**64**	**−119**	**77**	**16**
贷方 Credit		502	608	705	856	922	1 264	1 543
借方 Debit		545	488	572	792	1 041	1 188	1 526
A.货物和服务差额 **Goods and Services Balance**		**−49**	**107**	**116**	**50**	**−118**	**74**	**120**
贷方 Credit		478	574	659	788	866	1 189	1 472
借方 Debit		528	467	543	738	983	1 116	1 353
a.货物差额 Goods Balance		−56	92	87	52	−107	73	181
贷方 Credit		432	515	589	696	757	1 026	1 281
借方 Debit		488	424	502	644	863	953	1 101
b.服务差额 Services Balance		7	15	29	−2	−11	1	−61
贷方 Credit		46	59	70	92	109	164	191
借方 Debit		39	44	41	94	120	163	252
B.收益差额 **Income Balance**		**2**	**11**	**8**	**2**	**−13**	**−10**	**−118**
贷方 Credit		19	30	37	56	44	57	52
借方 Debit		17	20	29	53	57	68	170
C.经常转移差额 **Current Transfers Balance**		**4**	**3**	**8**	**12**	**12**	**13**	**14**
贷方 Credit		5	4	9	12	13	18	18
借方 Debit		1	1	1	1	1	4	4
二、资本和金融项目差额 **Capital and Financial Account Balance**		**64**	**−28**	**46**	**−3**	**235**	**326**	**387**
贷方 Credit		212	204	203	302	508	618	677
借方 Debit		148	232	157	305	274	291	290
A.资本账户差额 **Capital Account Balance**		**0**	**0**	**0**	**0**	**0**	**0**	**0**
贷方 Credit		0	0	0	0	0	0	0
借方 Debit		0	0	0	0	0	0	0
B.金融账户差额 **Financial Account Balance**		**64**	**−28**	**46**	**−3**	**235**	**326**	**387**
贷方 Credit		212	204	203	302	508	618	677
借方 Debit		148	232	157	305	274	291	290

单位：亿美元
Unit: USD 100 million

项目 年份 Item Year	1989	1990	1991	1992	1993	1994	1995
1.直接投资差额 Direct Investment Balance	26	27	35	72	231	318	338
贷方 Credit	34	35	44	112	275	338	377
借方 Debit	8	8	9	40	44	20	39
2.证券投资差额 Portfolio Investment Balance	−2	−2	2	−1	31	35	8
贷方 Credit	1	0	6	9	50	45	18
借方 Debit	3	2	3	9	20	10	10
3.其他投资差额 Other Investment Balance	40	−52	9	−74	−27	−27	40
贷方 Credit	177	169	154	182	183	235	282
借方 Debit	137	221	145	256	210	262	241
三、储备资产变动额 Reserve Assets	**−22**	**−61**	**−111**	**21**	**−18**	**−305**	**−225**
贷方 Credit	1	0	0	24	1	0	0
借方 Debit	23	61	111	3	18	305	225
其中：外汇储备差额 Foreign Exchange Reserves	−22	−55	−106	23	−18	−304	−220
四、净误差与遗漏 Net Errors and Omissions	**1**	**−31**	**−68**	**−83**	**−98**	**−98**	**−178**

中国国际收支概览表（3）

China's Balance of Payments Abridged（3）

项目 Item / 年份 Year	1996	1997	1998	1999	2000	2001	2002
一、经常账户差额 Current Account Balance	72	370	315	211	205	174	354
贷方 Credit	1 814	2 184	2 177	2 347	2 990	3 179	3 875
借方 Debit	1 741	1 815	1 862	2 135	2 785	3 005	3 521
A.货物和服务差额 Goods and Services Balance	176	428	438	306	289	281	374
贷方 Credit	1 717	2 072	2 074	2 210	2 796	2 994	3 654
借方 Debit	1 541	1 644	1 636	1 903	2 507	2 713	3 280
a.货物差额 Goods Balance	195	462	466	360	345	340	442
贷方 Credit	1 511	1 827	1 835	1 947	2 491	2 661	3 257
借方 Debit	1 315	1 364	1 369	1 587	2 147	2 321	2 815
b.服务差额 Services Balance	−20	−34	−28	−53	−56	−59	−68
贷方 Credit	206	246	239	262	304	333	397
借方 Debit	226	280	267	316	360	393	465
B.收益差额 Income Balance	−124	−110	−166	−145	−147	−192	−149
贷方 Credit	73	57	56	83	126	94	83
借方 Debit	198	167	222	228	272	286	233
C.经常转移差额 Current Transfers Balance	21	51	43	49	63	85	130
贷方 Credit	24	55	47	54	69	91	138
借方 Debit	2	3	4	4	5	6	8
二、资本和金融项目差额 Capital and Financial Account Balance	400	210	−63	52	19	348	323
贷方 Credit	710	926	893	918	920	995	1 283
借方 Debit	310	716	956	866	901	648	960
A.资本账户差额 Capital Account Balance	0	0	0	0	0	1	0
贷方 Credit	0	0	0	0	0	0	0
借方 Debit	0	0	0	0	0	1	0
B.金融账户差额 Financial Account Balance	400	210	−63	52	20	348	323
贷方 Credit	710	926	893	918	920	995	1 283
借方 Debit	310	716	956	865	900	647	960

单位：亿美元
Unit: USD 100 million

项目 年份 Item Year	1996	1997	1998	1999	2000	2001	2002
1.直接投资差额 Direct Investment Balance	381	417	411	370	375	374	468
贷方 Credit	424	454	456	410	421	471	531
借方 Debit	43	38	45	40	46	97	63
2.证券投资差额 Portfolio Investment Balance	17	69	−37	−112	−40	−194	−103
贷方 Credit	34	92	19	18	78	94	23
借方 Debit	16	23	56	130	118	285	126
3.其他投资差额 Other Investment Balance	2	−276	−437	−205	−315	169	−41
贷方 Credit	253	380	418	489	421	695	730
借方 Debit	251	655	854	695	736	526	771
三、储备资产变动额 Reserve Assets	−317	−357	−64	−85	−105	−473	−755
贷方 Credit	0	0	1	13	6	0	2
借方 Debit	317	357	65	98	111	473	757
其中：外汇储备差额 Foreign Exchange Reserves	−315	−349	−51	−97	−109	−466	−742
四、净误差与遗漏 Net Errors and Omissions	−155	−223	−187	−178	−119	−49	78

中国国际收支概览表（4）

China's Balance of Payments Abridged (4)

项目 Item 年份 Year	2003	2004	2005	2006	2007	2008
一、经常账户差额 Current Account Balance	**431**	**689**	**1 324**	**2 318**	**3 532**	**4 206**
贷方 Credit	5 196	7 032	9 039	11 478	14 684	17 462
借方 Debit	4 766	6 342	7 715	9 160	11 152	13 256
A.货物和服务差额 Goods and Services Balance	**358**	**512**	**1 246**	**2 089**	**3 080**	**3 488**
贷方 Credit	4 850	6 583	8 369	10 617	13 423	15 818
借方 Debit	4 492	6 071	7 123	8 528	10 342	12 330
a.货物差额 Goods Balance	444	590	1 342	2 177	3 159	3 606
贷方 Credit	4 383	5 934	7 625	9 697	12 201	14 347
借方 Debit	3 939	5 344	6 283	7 519	9 041	10 741
b.服务差额 Services Balance	−85	−78	−96	−88	−79	−118
贷方 Credit	468	649	744	920	1 222	1 471
借方 Debit	553	727	840	1 008	1 301	1 589
B.收益差额 Income Balance	**−102**	**−51**	**−161**	**−51**	**80**	**286**
贷方 Credit	161	206	393	546	835	1 118
借方 Debit	263	257	554	597	754	832
C.经常转移差额 Current Transfers Balance	**174**	**229**	**239**	**281**	**371**	**432**
贷方 Credit	185	243	277	316	426	526
借方 Debit	10	14	39	35	55	94
二、资本和金融项目差额 Capital and Financial Account Balance	**549**	**1 082**	**953**	**493**	**942**	**401**
贷方 Credit	2 432	3 984	4 851	7 346	9 936	9 845
借方 Debit	1 883	2 903	3 897	6 853	8 994	9 444
A.资本账户差额 Capital Account Balance	**0**	**−1**	**41**	**40**	**31**	**31**
贷方 Credit	0	0	42	41	33	33
借方 Debit	0	1	1	1	2	3
B.金融账户差额 Financial Account Balance	**549**	**1 082**	**912**	**453**	**911**	**371**
贷方 Credit	2 432	3 984	4 809	7 305	9 903	9 812
借方 Debit	1 883	2 902	3 897	6 852	8 992	9 441

单位：亿美元
Unit: USD 100 million

项目 年份 Item Year	2003	2004	2005	2006	2007	2008
1.直接投资差额 Direct Investment Balance	494	601	904	1 001	1 391	1 148
贷方 Credit	579	681	1 112	1 333	1 694	1 868
借方 Debit	85	80	208	331	303	720
2.证券投资差额 Portfolio Investment Balance	114	197	−47	−684	164	349
贷方 Credit	173	347	261	497	771	872
借方 Debit	59	150	308	1 181	606	524
3.其他投资差额 Other Investment Balance	−60	283	56	136	−644	−1 126
贷方 Credit	1 680	2 956	3 437	5 475	7 439	7 072
借方 Debit	1 739	2 672	3 381	5 340	8 083	8 198
三、储备资产变动额 Reserve Assets	−1 061	−1 901	−2 506	−2 848	−4 607	−4 795
贷方 Credit	3	5	19	6	5	1
借方 Debit	1 064	1 905	2 526	2 854	4 612	4 796
其中：外汇储备差额 Foreign Exchange Reserves	−1 060	−1 904	−2 526	−2 853	−4 609	−4 783
四、净误差与遗漏 Net Errors and Omissions	82	130	229	36	133	188

中国国际收支概览表（5）

China's Balance of Payments Abridged (5)

项目　年份 Item　Year	2009	2010	2011	2012	2013
一、经常账户差额 Current Account Balance	**2 433**	**2 378**	**1 361**	**2 154**	**1 482**
贷方 Credit	14 842	19 355	22 897	24 665	2 6621
借方 Debit	12 409	16 977	21 536	22 511	2 5139
A.货物和服务差额 Goods and Services Balance	**2 201**	**2 230**	**1 819**	**2 318**	**2 354**
贷方 Credit	13 333	17 436	20 898	22 483	24 250
借方 Debit	11 131	15 206	19 079	20 165	21 896
a.货物差额 Goods Balance	2 495	2 542	2 435	3 216	3 599
贷方 Credit	12 038	15 814	19 038	20 569	22 190
借方 Debit	9 543	13 272	16 603	17 353	18 591
b.服务差额 Services Balance	−294	−312	−616	−897	−1 245
贷方 Credit	1 295	1 622	1 860	1 914	2 060
借方 Debit	1 589	1 933	2 477	2 812	3 305
B.收益差额 Income Balance	**−85**	**−259**	**−703**	**−199**	**−784**
贷方 Credit	1 083	1 424	1 443	1 670	1 840
借方 Debit	1 168	1 683	2 146	1 869	2 624
C.经常转移差额 Current Transfers Balance	**317**	**407**	**245**	**34**	**−87**
贷方 Credit	426	495	556	512	532
借方 Debit	110	88	311	477	619
二、资本和金融项目差额 Capital and Financial Account Balance	**1 985**	**2 869**	**2 655**	**−318**	**3 461**
贷方 Credit	8 634	11 667	14 495	13 520	17 528
借方 Debit	6 649	8 798	11 840	13 838	14 067
A.资本账户差额 Capital Account Balance	**39**	**46**	**54**	**43**	**31**
贷方 Credit	42	48	56	45	45
借方 Debit	3	2	2	3	14
B.金融账户差额 Financial Account Balance	**1 945**	**2 822**	**2 600**	**−360**	**3 430**
贷方 Credit	8 592	11 618	14 439	13 475	17 483
借方 Debit	6 647	8 796	11 838	13 835	14 053

单位：亿美元
Unit: USD 100 million

项目　年份 Item　Year	2009	2010	2011	2012	2013
1.直接投资差额 Direct Investment Balance	872	1 857	2 317	1 763	2 180
贷方 Credit	1 671	2 730	3 316	2 956	3 806
借方 Debit	799	872	999	1 194	1 626
2.证券投资差额 Portfolio Investment Balance	271	240	196	478	529
贷方 Credit	1 102	636	519	829	1 058
借方 Debit	831	395	323	352	529
3.其他投资差额 Other Investment Balance	803	724	87	−2 601	722
贷方 Credit	5 820	8 253	10 603	9 689	12 619
借方 Debit	5 017	7 528	10 516	12 290	11 897
三、储备资产变动额 Reserve Assets	−4 003	−4 717	−3 878	−966	−4 314
贷方 Credit	1	0	10	136	13
借方 Debit	4 005	4 717	3 888	1 101	4 327
其中：外汇储备差额 Foreign Exchange Reserves	−3 821	−4 696	−3 848	−987	−4 327
四、净误差与遗漏 Net Errors and Omissions	−414	−529	−138	−871	−629

中国国际收支概览表（6）

China's Balance of Payments Abridged (6)

项目　年份 Item　Year	2014
一、经常账户差额 Current Account Balance	**2 197**
贷方 Credit	27 992
借方 Debit	25 795
A.货物和服务差额 Goods and Services Balance	**2 840**
贷方 Credit	25 451
借方 Debit	22 611
a.货物差额 Goods Balance	4 760
贷方 Credit	23 541
借方 Debit	18 782
b.服务差额 Services Balance	−1 920
贷方 Credit	1 909
借方 Debit	3 829
B.收益差额 Income Balance	**−341**
贷方 Credit	2 130
借方 Debit	2 471
C.经常转移差额 Current Transfers Balance	**−302**
贷方 Credit	411
借方 Debit	714
二、资本和金融项目差额 Capital and Financial Account Balance	**382**
贷方 Credit	25 730
借方 Debit	25 347
A.资本账户差额 Capital Account Balance	**−0**
贷方 Credit	19
借方 Debit	20

单位：亿美元
Unit: USD 100 million

项目 年份 Item Year	2014
B.金融账户差额 **Financial Account Balance**	**383**
贷方 Credit	25 710
借方 Debit	25 328
1.直接投资差额 Direct Investment Balance	2 087
贷方 Credit	4 352
借方 Debit	2 266
2.证券投资差额 Portfolio Investment Balance	824
贷方 Credit	1 664
借方 Debit	840
3.其他投资差额 Other Investment Balance	−2 528
贷方 Credit	19 694
借方 Debit	22 222
三、储备资产变动额 **Reserve Assets**	**−1 178**
贷方 Credit	312
借方 Debit	1 490
其中：外汇储备差额 Foreign Exchange Reserves	−1 188
四、净误差与遗漏 **Net Errors and Omissions**	**−1 401**

2014年中国国际收支平衡表

China's Balance of Payments in 2014

项目 Item	差额 Balance	贷方 Credit	借方 Debit
一、经常项目 Current Account	2 197	27 992	25 795
A. 货物和服务 Goods and Services	2 840	25 451	22 611
a.货物 Goods	4 760	23 541	18 782
b.服务 Services	−1 920	1 909	3 829
1.运输 Transportation	−579	382	962
2.旅游 Travel	−1 079	569	1 649
3.通信服务 Communication Services	−5	18	23
4.建筑服务 Construction Services	105	154	49
5.保险服务 Insurance Services	−179	46	225
6.金融服务 Financial Services	−4	45	49
7.计算机和信息服务 Computer and Information Services	99	184	85
8.专有权利使用费和特许费 Royalties and Licensing Fees	−219	7	226
9.咨询 Consulting Service	164	429	265
10.广告、宣传 Advertising and Public Opinion Polling	12	50	38
11.电影、音像 Audio−visual and Related Services	−7	2	9
12.其他商业服务 Other Business Services	−217	14	231
13.别处未提及的政府服务 Government Services, n.i.e	−10	11	20
B. 收益 Income	−341	2 130	2 471
1.职工报酬 Compensation of Employee	258	299	42
2.投资收益 Investment Income	−599	1 831	2 429
C. 经常转移 Current Transfers	−302	411	714
1.各级政府 General Government	−29	16	46
2.其他部门 Other Sectors	−273	395	668
二、资本和金融项目 Capital and Financial Account	382	25 730	25 347
A. 资本项目 Capital Account	−0	19	20
B. 金融项目 Financial Account	383	25 710	25 328
1. 直接投资 Direct Investment	2 087	4 352	2 266
1.1 我国在外直接投资 Abroad	−804	555	1 359
1.2 外国在华直接投资 In China	2 891	3 797	906
2. 证券投资 Portfolio Investment	824	1 664	840
2.1 资产 Assets	−108	293	401
2.1.1 股本证券 Equity Securities	−14	170	184
2.1.2 债务证券 Debt Securities	−94	123	217
2.1.2.1 (中)长期债券 Bonds and Notes	−92	123	215
2.1.2.2 货币市场工具 Money Market Instruments	−2	0	2
2.2 负债 Liabilities	932	1 371	439
2.2.1 股本证券 Equity Securities	519	777	258

单位：亿美元
Unit: USD 100 million

项目 Item	差额 Balance	贷方 Credit	借方 Debit
2.2.2 债务证券 Debt Securities	413	594	181
2.2.2.1 (中)长期债券 Bonds and Notes	410	497	88
2.2.2.2 货币市场工具 Money Market Instruments	4	97	94
3．其他投资 Other Investment	−2 528	19 694	22 222
3.1 资产 Assets	−3 030	995	4 025
3.1.1 贸易信贷 Trade Credits	−688	282	970
长期 Long−term	−14	6	19
短期 Short−term	−674	276	950
3.1.2 贷款 Loans	−738	177	915
长期 Long−term	−455	0	455
短期 Short−term	−282	177	459
3.1.3 货币和存款 Currency and Deposits	−1 597	514	2 111
3.1.4 其他资产 Other Assets	−8	22	29
长期 Long−term	0	0	0
短期 Short−term	−8	22	29
3.2 负债 Liabilities	502	18 699	18 197
3.2.1 贸易信贷 Trade Credits	−21	154	174
长期 Long−term	−0	3	3
短期 Short−term	−20	151	171
3.2.2 贷款 Loans	−343	17 464	17 807
长期 Long−term	−57	511	569
短期 Short−term	−286	16 953	17 239
3.2.3 货币和存款 Currency and Deposits	814	994	180
3.2.4 其他负债 Other Liabilities	52	87	35
长期 Long−term	58	64	6
短期 Short−term	−6	23	29
三、储备资产 Reserve Assets	−1 178	312	1 490
3.1 货币黄金 Monetary Gold	0	0	0
3.2 特别提款权 Special Drawing Rights	1	1	1
3.3 在国际货币基金组织的储备头寸 Reserve Position in the Fund	10	13	4
3.4 外汇 Foreign Exchange	−1 188	298	1 486
3.5 其他债权 Other Claims	0	0	0
四、净误差与遗漏 Net Errors and Omissions	−1 401	245	1646

美国国际收支概览表

Balance of Payments Abridged of United States

项目 Item	年份 Year	2007	2008	2009	2010	2011	2012	2013	2014
一、经常项目差额 Current Account Balance		−713.35	−681.34	−381.64	−449.48	−457.73	−440.42	−379.28	−410.63
贷方 Credit		2 569.75	2 752.25	2 283.01	2 622.80	2 981.37	3 100.04	3 178.73	3 291.35
借方 Debit		3 283.11	3 433.59	2 664.65	3 072.28	3 439.10	3 540.46	3 558.01	3 701.98
A.货物和服务差额 Goods and Services Balance		−698.98	−702.30	−383.63	−499.35	−556.80	−534.61	−474.82	−504.72
贷方 Credit		1 654.69	1 842.83	1 580.90	1 846.19	2 114.75	2 212.47	2 272.58	2 344.53
借方 Debit		2 353.67	2 545.12	1 964.52	2 345.54	2 671.55	2 747.08	2 747.40	2 849.24
a.货物差额 Goods Balance		−821.20	−832.49	−509.75	−649.74	−743.56	−740.80	−703.26	−735.79
贷方 Credit		1 165.15	1 308.80	1 070.27	1 289.21	1 496.43	1 561.91	1 590.32	1 635.13
借方 Debit		1 986.35	2 141.29	1 580.03	1 938.95	2 239.99	2 302.71	2 293.57	2 370.92
b.服务差额 Services Balance		122.22	130.19	126.13	150.40	186.76	206.19	228.43	231.07
贷方 Credit		489.54	534.03	510.62	556.99	618.32	650.56	682.26	709.39
借方 Debit		367.32	403.84	384.50	406.59	431.56	444.37	453.83	478.32
B.初次收入差额 Primary Income Balance		100.60	146.14	123.58	177.66	232.64	223.92	228.77	217.90
贷方 Credit		844.04	823.71	614.38	684.92	767.58	783.24	795.22	819.70
借方 Debit		743.43	677.57	490.80	507.26	534.94	559.31	566.45	601.80
C.二次收入差额 Secondary Income Balance		−114.98	−125.19	−121.59	−127.79	−133.58	−129.74	−133.22	−123.82
贷方 Credit		71.03	85.71	87.73	91.69	99.04	104.33	110.93	127.12
借方 Debit		186.01	210.89	209.32	219.48	232.61	234.07	244.15	250.94
二、资本项目差额 Capital Account Balance		0.38	6.01	−0.14	−0.16	−1.21	6.96	−0.41	−0.05
三、金融项目净贷出（+）/净借入（−） Financial Account Net Lending(+)/Net Borrow(−)		−617.26	−730.57	−231.02	−438.04	−551.71	−439.35	−351.23	−141.65
1.直接投资差额 Direct Investment Balance		192.88	18.99	159.94	95.23	178.78	221.88	166.28	260.11
1.1资产 Assets		532.94	351.72	313.73	354.58	431.32	425.67	402.15	353.16
1.2负债 Liabilities		340.07	332.73	153.79	259.34	252.54	203.79	235.87	93.05
2.证券投资差额 Portfolio Investment Balance		−776.94	−809.40	17.76	−620.41	−245.87	−586.79	−46.25	−145.14

单位：10亿美元
Unit: USD billion

项目 Item	年份 Year	2007	2008	2009	2010	2011	2012	2013	2014
2.1资产 Assets		379.68	−285.72	375.11	200.02	78.20	157.60	427.18	547.41
2.2负债 Liabilities		1 156.61	523.69	357.35	820.44	324.07	744.39	473.43	692.55
3.金融衍生产品（储备除外）和雇员认股权差额 Derivatives (other than reserves) and Employee Stock Options Balance		−6.22	32.95	−44.82	−14.08	−35.01	7.06	1.85	−53.53
4.其他投资差额 Other Investment Balance		−27.10	22.05	−416.16	99.39	−465.49	−85.96	−470.01	−199.50
4.1资产 Assets		659.77	−380.32	−608.89	407.02	−50.78	−452.88	−230.74	−76.50
4.2负债 Liabilities		686.86	−402.37	−192.73	307.63	414.72	−366.92	239.27	123.01
5.储备资产差额 Reserve Assets Balance		0.12	4.85	52.26	1.84	15.88	4.46	−3.10	−3.58
四、净误差与遗漏 Net Errors and Omissions		95.71	−55.24	150.76	11.60	−92.77	−5.89	28.46	269.03

德国国际收支概览表

Balance of Payments Abridged of Germany

项目 Item 年份 Year	2007	2008	2009	2010	2011	2012	2013	2014
一、经常项目差额 Current Account Balance	248.78	226.27	198.35	212.16	247.22	255.38	273.97	290.00
贷方 Credit	1 886.89	2 022.77	1 643.34	1 824.31	2 131.23	2 026.88	2 095.53	2 110.00
借方 Debit	1 638.10	1 796.50	1 444.99	1 612.15	1 884.01	1 771.49	1 821.56	1 820.00
A.货物和服务差额 Goods and Services Balance	234.18	228.80	161.19	189.85	196.71	205.81	227.29	252.00
贷方 Credit	1 533.35	1 711.80	1 371.93	1 545.99	1 812.19	1 737.57	1 805.31	1 770.00
借方 Debit	1 299.17	1 483.00	1 210.74	1 356.14	1 615.47	1 531.76	1 578.02	1 520.00
a.货物差额 Goods Balance	272.82	267.78	182.22	209.35	222.96	233.97	257.79	304.00
贷方 Credit	1 300.21	1 446.50	1 123.24	1 286.70	1 526.67	1 461.84	1 506.33	1 490.00
借方 Debit	1 027.40	1 178.72	941.01	1 077.36	1 303.72	1 227.87	1 248.54	1 190.00
b.服务差额 Services Balance	−38.64	38.98	−21.03	−19.50	−26.25	−28.16	−30.50	−51.96
贷方 Credit	233.13	265.31	248.70	259.29	285.51	275.73	298.98	278.00
借方 Debit	271.77	304.28	269.73	278.79	311.76	303.89	329.48	330.00
B.初次收入差额 Primary Income Balance	59.06	46.27	83.09	73.41	97.44	98.22	102.42	87.83
贷方 Credit	328.31	283.49	247.17	255.16	291.22	264.70	261.76	259.00
借方 Debit	269.25	237.22	164.07	181.75	193.78	166.48	159.34	172.00
C.二次收入差额 Secondary Income Balance	−44.46	−48.79	−45.94	−51.10	−46.94	−48.64	−55.74	−49.70
贷方 Credit	25.23	27.48	24.24	23.16	27.83	24.61	28.45	76.88
借方 Debit	69.69	76.27	70.18	74.26	74.76	73.26	84.20	127.00
二、资本项目差额 Capital Account Balance	0.07	−0.18	0.01	−0.74	0.85	0.02	2.42	3.92
三、金融项目净贷出（+）/ 净借入（−） Financial Account Net Lending(+)/Net Borrow(−)	290.73	255.87	221.95	166.33	242.88	286.39	333.23	324.00
1.直接投资差额 Direct Investment Balance	91.14	68.36	44.13	61.53	21.40	66.48	30.07	110.00
1.1资产 Assets	120.00	84.89	81.90	96.79	66.08	101.18	62.70	119.00
1.2负债 Liabilities	28.86	16.53	37.77	35.26	44.68	34.71	32.63	8.39
2.证券投资差额 Portfolio Investment Balance	−215.36	−44.54	119.24	154.11	−42.57	83.42	218.62	168.00

单位：10亿美元
Unit: USD billion

项目 Item	年份 Year	2007	2008	2009	2010	2011	2012	2013	2014
2.1资产 Assets		198.95	−14.74	110.19	230.22	29.50	141.58	186.67	199.00
2.2负债 Liabilities		414.32	29.80	−9.04	76.11	72.07	58.16	−31.95	30.97
3.金融衍生产品（储备除外）和雇员认股权差额 Derivatives (other than reserves) and Employee Stock Options Balance		119.86	48.05	−13.80	22.94	38.56	20.86	21.40	42.27
3.1资产 Assets		0	0	0	0	0	0	0	0
3.2负债 Liabilities		−119.86	−48.05	13.80	−22.94	−38.56	−20.86	−21.40	−42.27
4.其他投资差额 Other Investment Balance		293.87	181.22	76.94	−74.41	221.57	113.95	61.98	6.54
4.1资产 Assets		455.26	221.78	−130.24	160.23	196.68	217.52	−247.83	40.43
4.2负债 Liabilities		161.40	40.56	−207.18	234.64	−24.88	103.57	−309.81	33.90
5.储备资产差额 Reserve Assets Balance		1.23	2.78	−4.56	2.16	3.92	1.68	1.16	−3.32
四、净误差与遗漏 Net Errors and Omissions		41.87	29.78	23.60	−45.09	−5.19	30.99	56.84	29.69

英国国际收支概览表

Balance of Payments Abridged of United Kingdom

项目 Item / 年份 Year	2007	2008	2009	2010	2011	2012	2013	2014
一、经常项目差额 Current Account Balance	−71.08	−41.16	−37.05	−75.23	−32.76	−94.27	−111.08	−161.4
贷方 Credit	1 344.92	1 281.56	891.45	929.55	1 111.47	1 050.11	1 028.05	1 110.82
借方 Debit	1 416.00	1 322.72	928.50	1 004.78	1 144.23	1 144.38	1 139.14	1 272.22
A.货物和服务差额 Goods and Services Balance	−94.21	−89.31	−54.92	−64.23	−47.05	−59.20	−50.33	−55.83
贷方 Credit	730.56	756.10	595.91	667.60	773.49	768.83	775.91	835.58
借方 Debit	824.77	845.40	650.83	731.83	820.54	828.03	826.24	891.41
a.货物差额 Goods Balance	−179.74	−173.46	−128.56	−152.45	160.65	−171.72	−168.58	−197
贷方 Credit	442.28	468.14	356.35	410.89	479.15	474.61	476.57	481.88
借方 Debit	622.02	641.60	484.91	563.34	639.80	646.34	645.15	678.88
b.服务差额 Services Balance	85.53	84.15	73.64	88.22	113.60	112.52	118.25	141.17
贷方 Credit	288.29	287.96	239.56	256.71	294.34	294.21	299.34	353.71
借方 Debit	202.76	203.81	165.93	168.49	180.75	181.69	181.09	212.53
B.初次收入差额 Primary Income Balance	50.25	74.64	40.66	20.68	49.38	0.39	−18.32	−63.89
贷方 Credit	586.56	495.41	269.06	240.13	311.65	254.61	226.73	242.85
借方 Debit	536.31	420.77	228.40	219.45	262.27	254.22	245.05	306.74
C.二次收入差额 Secondary Income Balance	−27.12	−26.49	−22.79	−31.68	−35.10	−35.46	−42.43	−41.68
贷方 Credit	27.80	30.06	26.48	21.82	26.32	26.67	25.41	32.39
借方 Debit	54.91	56.55	49.27	53.50	61.41	62.13	67.84	74.08
二、资本项目差额 Capital Account Balance	5.17	6.05	5.14	5.73	5.18	6.65	8.34	−0.35
三、金融项目净贷出（+）/ 净借入（−）Financial Account Net Lending(+)/Net Borrow(−)	−49.99	−44.17	−48.57	−64.38	−12.21	−102.18	−104.75	−153.88
1.直接投资差额 Direct Investment Balance	126.02	69.64	−30.06	−23.25	55.91	−10.95	−16.38	−131.69
1.1资产 Assets	366.56	331.17	−26.00	38.08	92.15	55.88	18.75	−103.94
1.2负债 Liabilities	240.54	261.54	4.06	61.33	36.24	66.83	35.13	27.76

单位：10亿美元
Unit: USD billion

项目 Item	年份 Year	2007	2008	2009	2010	2011	2012	2013	2014
2.证券投资差额 Portfolio Investment Balance		−256.13	−588.92	−38.33	2.16	72.28	294.10	−48.45	−169.01
2.1资产 Assets		179.74	−199.66	254.61	122.52	11.17	178.53	10.77	39.52
2.2负债 Liabilities		435.87	389.27	292.94	120.36	−61.11	−115.57	59.22	208.53
3.金融衍生产品（储备除外）和雇员认股权差额 Derivatives (other than reserves) and Employee Stock Options Balance		53.98	219.23	−49.08	−49.88	4.16	−47.16	−0.65	−23.75
3.1资产 Assets		0	0	0	0	0	0	0	0
3.2负债 Liabilities		−53.98	−219.23	49.08	49.88	−4.16	47.16	0.65	23.75
4.其他投资差额 Other Investment Balance		23.62	259.05	59.18	−2.70	−152.51	−350.26	−46.96	159.08
4.1资产 Assets		1 474.38	−981.60	−507.91	345.35	170.67	−385.70	−342.17	188.01
4.2负债 Liabilities		1 450.77	−1 240.65	−567.08	348.05	323.18	−35.44	−295.21	28.93
5.储备资产差额 Reserve Assets Balance		2.52	−3.17	9.73	9.28	7.95	12.09	7.69	11.5
四、净误差与遗漏 Net Errors and Omissions		15.91	−9.07	−16.66	5.11	15.37	−14.56	−2.02	7.87

巴西国际收支概览表

Balance of Payments Abridged of Brazil

项目 Item	年份 Year 2007	2008	2009	2010	2011	2012	2013	2014
一、经常项目差额 Current Account Balance	1.55	−28.19	−24.30	−47.27	−52.48	−54.25	−81.37	−103.98
贷方 Credit	201.07	246.22	194.28	245.69	309.92	297.96	296.84	281.93
借方 Debit	199.52	274.41	218.59	292.97	362.40	352.20	378.22	385.91
A.货物和服务差额 Goods and Services Balance	26.81	8.15	6.04	−10.69	−8.15	−21.64	−44.97	−54.54
贷方 Credit	184.60	228.39	180.72	233.51	294.25	282.44	281.30	264.81
借方 Debit	157.79	220.25	174.68	244.20	302.39	304.09	326.26	319.35
a.货物差额 Goods Balance	40.03	24.84	25.29	20.15	29.81	19.43	2.56	−6.25
贷方 Credit	160.65	197.94	152.99	201.92	256.04	242.58	242.18	224.64
借方 Debit	120.62	173.11	127.70	181.77	226.23	223.15	239.62	230.89
b.服务差额 Services Balance	−13.22	−16.69	−19.25	−30.84	−37.95	−41.08	−47.52	−48.29
贷方 Credit	23.95	30.45	27.73	31.60	38.21	39.86	39.12	40.17
借方 Debit	37.17	47.14	46.97	62.43	76.16	80.94	86.64	88.46
B.初次收入差额 Primary Income Balance	−29.29	−40.56	−33.68	−39.49	−47.32	−35.45	−39.77	−51.48
贷方 Credit	11.49	12.51	8.83	7.41	10.75	10.89	10.07	12.85
借方 Debit	40.78	53.07	42.51	46.89	58.07	46.34	49.84	64.33
C.二次收入差额 Secondary Income Balance	4.03	4.22	3.34	2.90	2.98	2.85	3.36	2.04
贷方 Credit	4.97	5.32	4.74	4.77	4.92	4.63	5.48	4.27
借方 Debit	0.94	1.09	1.40	1.87	1.93	1.78	2.11	2.24
二、资本项目差额 Capital Account Balance	0.76	1.06	1.13	1.12	1.57	−1.88	1.19	0.23
三、金融项目净贷出（+）/净借入（−）Financial Account Net Lending(+)/Net Borrow(−)	−0.85	−25.33	−23.52	−49.69	−52.18	−55.74	−79.35	−99.70
1.直接投资差额 Direct Investment Balance	−27.52	−24.60	−36.03	−36.92	−67.69	−68.09	−67.54	−71.11
1.1资产 Assets	17.06	26.12	−4.55	16.43	3.85	8.02	13.35	25.74

单位：10亿美元
Unit: USD billion

项目 年份 Item Year	2007	2008	2009	2010	2011	2012	2013	2014
1.2负债 Liabilities	44.58	50.72	31.48	53.34	71.54	76.11	80.89	96.85
2.证券投资差额 **Portfolio Investment Balance**	**−48.39**	**−1.13**	**−50.28**	**−63.01**	**−35.31**	**−8.27**	**−25.69**	**−37.89**
2.1资产 Assets	−0.29	−1.90	−4.12	4.78	−16.86	8.26	8.97	2.84
2.2负债 Liabilities	48.10	−0.77	46.16	67.79	18.45	16.53	34.66	40.73
3.金融衍生产品（储备除外）和雇员认股权差额 **Derivatives (other than reserves) and Employee Stock Options Balance**	**0.71**	**0.31**	**−0.16**	**0.11**	**0**	**−0.02**	**−0.11**	**1.57**
3.1资产 Assets	−0.09	−0.30	−0.32	−0.13	−0.25	−0.15	−0.38	−7.61
3.2负债 Liabilities	−0.80	−0.61	−0.17	−0.25	−0.25	−0.12	−0.27	−9.18
4.其他投资差额 **Other Investment Balance**	**−13.13**	**−2.87**	**16.30**	**1.02**	**−7.81**	**1.75**	**19.92**	**−3.10**
4.1资产 Assets	18.55	5.27	30.38	42.57	38.98	24.28	39.56	47.62
4.2负债 Liabilities	31.68	8.14	14.08	41.54	46.80	22.52	19.64	50.72
5.储备资产差额 **Reserve Assets Balance**	**87.48**	**2.97**	**46.65**	**49.10**	**58.64**	**18.90**	**−5.93**	**10.83**
四、净误差与遗漏 **Net Errors and Omissions**	**−3.15**	**1.81**	**−0.35**	**−3.54**	**−1.27**	**0.38**	**0.83**	**4.04**

俄罗斯国际收支概览表

Balance of Payments Abridged of Russia

项目 Item / 年份 Year	2007	2008	2009	2010	2011	2012	2013	2014
一、经常项目差额 Current Account Balance	72.19	103.94	50.38	67.45	97.27	71.28	32.76	59.46
贷方 Credit	442.19	592.60	382.72	487.16	629.90	653.99	652.75	628.19
借方 Debit	370.00	488.66	332.34	419.70	532.63	582.71	619.99	568.73
A.货物和服务差额 Goods and Services Balance	106.73	157.21	95.63	120.87	163.40	145.08	121.69	134.50
贷方 Credit	390.39	523.43	342.95	441.83	573.45	589.77	593.16	563.56
借方 Debit	283.66	366.23	247.32	320.96	410.05	444.70	471.47	429.06
a.货物差额 Goods Balance	123.45	177.63	113.23	146.99	196.85	191.66	180.31	189.74
贷方 Credit	346.53	466.30	297.15	392.67	515.41	527.43	523.29	497.76
借方 Debit	223.08	288.67	183.92	245.68	318.55	335.77	342.98	308.03
b.服务差额 Services Balance	−16.72	−20.42	−17.60	−26.12	−33.46	−46.59	−58.62	−55.24
贷方 Credit	43.86	57.14	45.80	49.16	58.04	62.34	69.87	65.80
借方 Debit	60.58	77.56	63.40	75.28	91.50	108.93	128.49	121.04
B.初次收入差额 Primary Income Balance	−28.83	−46.48	−39.74	−47.10	−60.40	−67.66	−79.76	−67.18
贷方 Credit	45.58	61.82	33.40	38.06	42.69	47.76	42.10	46.91
借方 Debit	74.41	108.30	73.14	85.17	103.09	115.42	121.86	114.09
C.二次收入差额 Secondary Income Balance	−5.71	−6.79	−5.51	−6.32	−5.72	−6.13	−9.17	−7.85
贷方 Credit	6.22	7.35	6.37	7.26	13.77	16.46	17.49	17.72
借方 Debit	11.93	14.13	11.88	13.58	19.49	22.59	26.66	25.58
二、资本项目差额 Capital Account Balance	−10.64	−0.10	−12.47	−0.04	0.13	−5.22	−0.41	−42.01
三、金融项目净贷出（+）/净借入（−） Financial Account Net Lending(+)/Net Borrow(−)	51.82	100.78	31.52	58.28	88.75	55.69	20.44	26.22
1.直接投资差额 Direct Investment Balance	−11.07	−19.12	6.70	9.45	11.77	−1.77	15.64	35.48
1.1资产 Assets	44.80	55.66	43.28	52.62	66.85	48.82	94.91	56.44
1.2负债 Liabilities	55.87	74.78	36.58	43.17	55.08	50.59	79.26	20.96

单位：10亿美元
Unit: USD billion

项目 Item	年份 Year	2007	2008	2009	2010	2011	2012	2013	2014
2.证券投资差额 **Portfolio Investment Balance**		**−4.86**	**35.69**	**1.88**	**1.50**	**15.28**	**−17.03**	**11.58**	**39.87**
2.1资产 Assets		10.54	7.77	10.60	3.44	9.84	2.28	11.94	16.74
2.2负债 Liabilities		15.39	−27.92	8.72	1.95	−5.44	19.31	0.36	−23.13
3.金融衍生产品（储备除外）和雇员认股权差额 **Derivatives (other than reserves) and Employee Stock Options Balance**		**−0.33**	**1.37**	**3.24**	**1.84**	**1.39**	**1.36**	**0.35**	**4.78**
3.1资产 Assets		−2.76	−9.12	−9.89	−8.84	−16.44	−16.70	−8.49	−16.58
3.2负债 Liabilities		−2.43	−10.49	−13.13	−10.68	−17.83	−18.05	−8.83	−21.36
4.其他投资差额 **Other Investment Balance**		**−80.85**	**121.76**	**16.32**	**8.74**	**47.68**	**43.12**	**14.94**	**53.64**
4.1资产 Assets		59.93	185.86	−9.24	19.23	83.37	83.70	76.59	26.50
4.2负债 Liabilities		140.78	64.10	−25.57	10.49	35.69	40.59	61.65	−27.14
5.储备资产差额 **Reserve Assets Balance**		**148.93**	**−38.92**	**3.38**	**36.75**	**12.63**	**30.02**	**−22.08**	**−107.55**
四、净误差与遗漏 **Net Errors and Omissions**		**−9.73**	**−3.05**	**−6.39**	**−9.14**	**−8.66**	**−10.37**	**−11.91**	**8.77**

中国国际投资头寸表

China´s International Investment Position

项目 Item	2007年末 End-2007	2008年末 End-2008	2009年末 End-2009	2010年末 End-2010	2011年末 End-2011	2012年末 End-2012	2013年末 End-2013	2014年末 End-2014
净头寸 Net	11 881	14 938	14 905	16 880	16 884	18 665	19 716	17 764
A.资产 Assets	24 162	29 567	34 369	41 189	47 345	52 132	59 368	64 087
1.在国外直接投资 Direct Investment Abroad	1 160	1 857	2 458	3 172	4 248	5 319	6 091	7 443
2.证券投资 Portfolio Investment	2 846	2 525	2 428	2 571	2 044	2 406	2 585	2 625
2.1股本证券 Equity Securities	196	214	546	630	864	1 298	1 530	1 613
2.2债务证券 Debt Securities	2 650	2 311	1 882	1 941	1 180	1 108	1 055	1 012
3.其他投资 Other Investment	4 683	5 523	4 952	6 304	8 495	10 527	11 888	15 026
3.1贸易信贷 Trade Credits	1 160	1 102	1 444	2 060	2 769	3 387	3 990	4 677
3.2贷款 Loans	888	1 071	974	1 174	2 232	2 778	3 089	3 747
3.3货币和存款 Currency and Deposits	1 380	1 529	1 310	2 051	2 942	3 906	3 772	5 541
3.4其他资产 Other Assets	1 255	1 821	1 224	1 018	552	457	1 038	1 061
4.储备资产 Reserve assets	15 473	19 662	24 532	29 142	32 558	33 879	38 804	38 993
4.1货币黄金 Monetary Gold	170	169	371	481	530	567	408	401
4.2特别提款权 Special Drawing Right	12	12	125	123	119	114	112	105
4.3在基金组织中的储备头寸 Reserve Position in the Fund	8	20	44	64	98	82	71	57
4.4外汇 Foreign Exchange	15 282	19 460	23 992	28 473	31 811	33 116	38 213	38 430

单位：亿美元
Unit: USD 100 million

项目 Item	2007年末 End−2007	2008年末 End−2008	2009年末 End−2009	2010年末 End−2010	2011年末 End−2011	2012年末 End−2012	2013年末 End−2013	2014年末 End−2014
B.负债 **Liabilities**	**12 281**	**14 629**	**19 464**	**24 308**	**30 461**	**33 467**	**39 652**	**46 323**
1.外国来华直接投资 Direct Investment in Reporting Economy	7 037	9 155	13 148	15 696	19 069	20 680	23 475	26 779
2.证券投资 Portfolio Investment	1 466	1 677	1 900	2 239	2 485	3 361	3 868	5 143
2.1股本证券 Equity Securities	1 290	1 505	1 748	2 061	2 114	2 619	2 980	3 693
2.2债务证券 Debt Securities	176	172	152	178	371	742	889	1 449
3.其他投资 Other Investment	3 778	3 796	4 416	6 373	8 907	9 426	12 309	14 402
3.1贸易信贷 Trade Credits	1 487	1 296	1 617	2 112	2 492	2 915	3 365	3 344
3.2贷款 Loans	1 033	1 030	1 636	2 389	3 724	3 680	5 642	5 720
3.3货币和存款 Currency and Deposits	791	918	937	1 650	2 477	2 446	3 051	5 030
3.4其他负债 Other Liabilities	467	552	227	222	214	384	252	308

外汇储备

Foreign Exchange Reserves

单位：亿美元
Unit: USD 100 million

年份 Year	外汇储备余额 Foreign Exchange Reserves	外汇储备增加额 Increase of Foreign Exchange Reserves
1990	111	55
1991	217	106
1992	194	−23
1993	212	18
1994	516	304
1995	736	220
1996	1 050	315
1997	1 399	348
1998	1 450	51
1999	1 547	97
2000	1 656	109
2001	2 122	466
2002	2 864	742
2003	4 033	1 168
2004	6 099	2 067
2005	8 189	2 090
2006	10 663	2 475
2007	15 282	4 619
2008	19 460	4 178
2009	23 992	4 531
2010	28 473	4 481
2011	31 811	3 338
2012	33 116	1 304
2013	38 213	5 097
2014	38 430	217

月度外汇储备余额及其变动情况
Change of Monthly Foreign Exchange Reserves

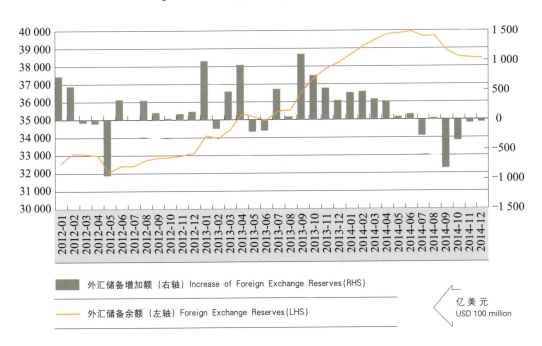

　外汇储备增加额（右轴）Increase of Foreign Exchange Reserves（RHS）

　外汇储备余额（左轴）Foreign Exchange Reserves（LHS）

亿 美 元
USD 100 million

2014 年末部分国家和地区外汇储备
Foreign Reserves of Some Countries/Regions，End—2014

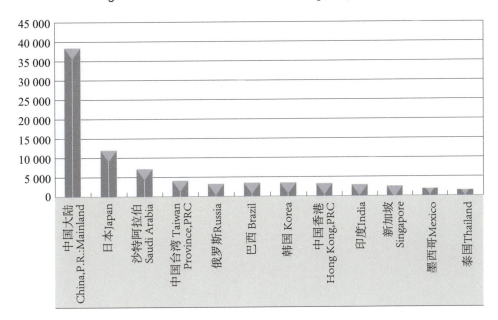

亿 美 元
USD 100 million

二、对外贸易①

II. Foreign Trade

2014年世界货物贸易出口前十名

Top 10 Countries／Regions of Goods Export in 2014

国家/地区 Countries/Regions	出口额（10亿美元） Export（USD billion）	增长 Increase（%）	占世界出口总额比重 Ratio to total export of the world（%）	2014年排名 Ranking in 2014
世界World	18 935	0.8	100	
1.中国PRC	2 343	6.1	12.4	1
2.美国USA	1 623	2.8	8.6	2
3.德国Germany	1 511	4.0	8.0	3
4.日本Japan	684	−4.3	3.6	4
5.荷兰Netherlands	672	1.2	3.6	5
6.法国France	583	0.5	3.1	6
7.韩国Korea	573	2.3	3.0	7
8.意大利Italy	529	2.1	2.8	11
9.中国香港HongKong,China	524	−2.2	2.8	9
10.英国UK	507	−6.3	2.7	8

①数据来源：海关总署、世界贸易组织相关资料。
Sources：General Administration of Customs；World Trade Organization.

2014年世界货物贸易进口前十名

Top 10 Countries/Regions of Goods Import in 2014

国家/地区 Countries/Regions	进口额（10亿美元） Import（USD billion）	增长 Increase（%）	占世界进口总额比重 Ratio to total Import of the world（%）	2014年排名 Ranking in 2014
世界World	19 024	0.8	100	
1.美国USA	2 409	3.3	12.7	1
2.中国PRC	1 960	0.5	10.3	2
3.德国Germany	1 217	2.5	6.4	3
4.日本Japan	822	−1.3	4.3	4
5.英国UK	683	4.4	3.6	6
6.法国France	679	−0.3	3.6	5
7.中国香港HongKong,China	601	−3.4	3.2	7
8.荷兰Netherlands	587	−0.5	3.1	8
9.韩国Korea	526	1.9	2.8	9
10.加拿大Canada	475	0.2	2.5	11

中国进出口总值

China's Total Value of Import & Export

单位：亿美元
Unit: USD 100 million

年度 Year	进出口 Import & Export	出口 Export	进口 Import	差额 Balance
1981	440	220	220	0
1982	416	223	193	30
1983	436	222	214	8
1984	535	261	274	−13
1985	696	274	423	−149
1986	738	309	429	−120
1987	827	394	432	−38
1988	1 028	475	553	−78
1989	1 117	525	591	−66
1990	1 154	621	534	87
1991	1 357	719	638	81
1992	1 655	849	806	44
1993	1 957	917	1 040	−122
1994	2 366	1 210	1 156	54
1995	2 809	1 488	1 321	167
1996	2 899	1 511	1 388	122
1997	3 252	1 828	1 424	404
1998	3 239	1 837	1 402	435
1999	3 606	1 949	1 657	292
2000	4 743	2 492	2 251	241
2001	5 097	2 661	2 436	226
2002	6 208	3 256	2 952	304
2003	8 510	4 382	4 128	255
2004	11 546	5 933	5 612	321
2005	14 219	7 620	6 600	1 020
2006	17 604	9 689	7 915	1 775
2007	21 766	12 205	9 561	2 643
2008	25 633	14 307	11 326	2 981
2009	22 072	12 017	10 059	1 957
2010	29 728	15 779	13 948	1 831
2011	36 421	18 986	17 435	1 551
2012	38 668	20 489	18 178	2 311
2013	41 603	22 100	19 503	2 598
2014	43 030	23 427	19 603	3 825

进出口增长率
Growth Rate of Import & Export

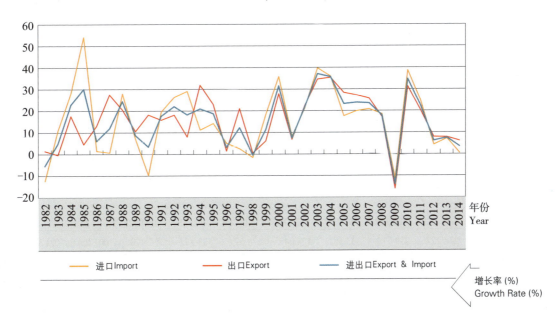

月度进口、出口和进出口差额
Monthly Import、Export、Import & Export Balance

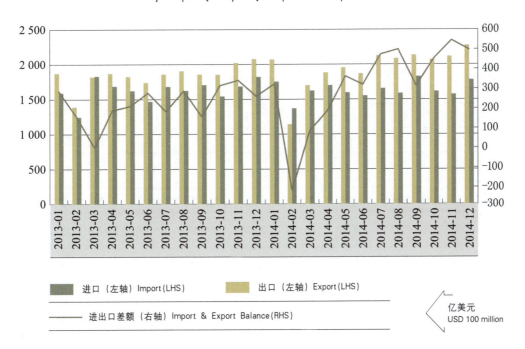

按贸易方式分类进出口

Import & Export by Trading Forms

贸易方式Trading Forms	2004	2005	2006	2007	2008	2009	2010	2011	2012	2013	2014
进口Import	**561 423**	**660 118**	**791 614**	**955 818**	**1 133 086**	**1 005 555**	**1 394 829**	**1 743 458**	**1 817 826**	**1 950 289**	**1 960 290**
一般贸易 Ordinary Trade	248 227	279 719	333 181	428 648	572 677	533 872	767 978	1 007 464	1 021 819	1 109 718	1 109 513
国家间、国际组织间无偿援助和捐赠的物资 Foreign Aid and Donation by Overseas	98	49	65	35	49	43	22	16	27	21	38
其他捐赠物资 Other Donations	12	19	22	10	58	136	185	266	338	11	10
来料加工装配贸易 Processing and Assembling Trade	53 721	67 029	73 834	89 165	90 162	75 993	99 295	93 635	84 459	87 543	97 537
进料加工贸易 Processing with Imported Materials	168 020	206 997	247 662	279 228	288 243	246 345	318 134	376 161	396 710	409 447	426 843
寄售代销贸易 Goods on Consignment	8	6	3	2	2	2	2	2	1	0	0
边境小额贸易 Border trade	5 043	5 721	6 214	7 589	8 975	7 196	9 634	14 448	15 289	14 065	9 856
加工贸易进口设备 Equipment Imported for Processing & Assembling	2 603	2 862	2 817	3 277	2 859	953	1 212	885	912	969	687
租赁贸易 Goods on Lease	2 223	3 681	8 067	8 280	6 932	3 448	5 628	5 459	6 760	8 656	10 212
外商投资企业作为投资进口的设备物品 Equipment or Materials Imported as Investment by Foreign-invested Enterprises	31 203	27 674	27 823	25 906	27 677	15 176	16 312	17 508	13 429	9 835	9 059
出料加工贸易 Outward Processing Trade	24	33	33	39	160	78	126	73	236	252	307
易货贸易 Barter Trade	13	3	6	4	1	8	1	2	0	1	3
免税外汇商品 Duty Free Commodities on Payment of Foreign Exchange	6	8	6	6	6	5	10	13	26	28	20
保税监管场所进出境货物 Customs Warehousing Trade	11 081	20 065	32 018	41 720	57 277	54 392	61 099	79 658	83 969	84 844	99 870
海关特殊监管区域物流货物 Entrepot Trade by Bonded Area	37 720	44 255	55 508	66 910	73 739	64 259	109 241	140 831	185 132	218 448	186 689
海关特殊监管区域进口设备 Equipment Imported into Export Processing Zone	882	1 411	3 623	4 108	3 118	2 113	3 994	4 741	6 094	3 993	5 133
其他 Others	539	586	732	890	1 150	1 535	1 957	2 296	2 624	2 458	2 950
出口 **Export**	**593 368**	**761 999**	**969 073**	**1 218 015**	**1 428 546**	**1 201 663**	**1 577 932**	**1 898 600**	**2 048 935**	**2 210 042**	**2 342 747**

贸易方式 Trading Forms	2004	2005	2006	2007	2008	2009	2010	2011	2012	2013	2014
一般贸易 Ordinary Trade	243 635	315 091	416 318	538 576	662 584	529 833	720 733	917 124	988 007	1 087 553	1 203 682
国家间、国际组织间无偿援助和捐赠的物资 Foreign Aid and Donation by overseas	187	225	211	201	231	291	294	471	551	456	478
其他捐赠物资 Other Donations	0	0	0	0	2	8	3	11	2	8	6
补偿贸易 Compensation Trade	9	0	1	0	0	0	0	0	0	0	0
来料加工装配贸易 Processing and Assembling Trade	68 569	83 970	94 483	116 043	110 520	93 423	112 317	107 653	98 866	92 479	90 692
进料加工贸易 Processing with Imported Materials	259 419	332 511	415 892	501 613	564 663	493 558	628 017	727 763	763 913	768 337	793 668
寄售代销贸易 Goods on Consignment	1	1	2	4	4	6	1	2	4	1	0
边境小额贸易 Border trade	4 431	7 409	9 943	13 739	21 904	13 667	16 408	20 203	24 216	30 929	37 207
对外承包工程出口货物 Contracting Projects	1 130	1 705	3 071	5 188	10 963	13 357	12 617	14 923	14 782	16 011	16 326
租赁贸易 Goods on Lease	15	90	214	84	189	117	145	166	562	305	327
出料加工贸易 Outward Processing Trade	27	27	24	44	118	46	185	198	196	199	235
易货贸易 Barter Trade	28	17	19	48	16	1	1	1	1	2	3
保税监管场所进出境货物 Customs Warehousing Trade	5 739	7 956	13 069	18 624	28 404	26 793	35 366	43 294	42 477	46 510	53 288
海关特殊监管区域物流货物 Entrepot Trade by Bonded Area	9 354	11 615	14 463	20 977	23 937	21 476	36 502	49 655	94 819	141 990	110 395
其他 Others	824	1 380	1 361	2 916	5 011	9 088	1 5343	1 7135	20 540	25 262	36 438

按企业类型分类进出口

单位：亿美元
Unit: USD 100 million

Import & Export by Type of Enterprises

企业类型 Type of Enterprises	2004	2005	2006	2007	2008	2009	2010	2011	2012	2013	2014
进口 Import	**5 614**	**6 601**	**7 916**	**9 558**	**11 331**	**10 056**	**13 948**	**17 435**	**18 178**	**19 503**	**19 603**
国有企业 State-owned Enterprises	1 765	1 972	2 252	2 697	3 538	2 885	3 876	4 934	4 954	4 990	4 911
外商投资企业 Foreign-funded Enterprises	3 246	3 875	4 726	5 594	6 200	5 452	7 380	8 648	8 712	8 748	9 093
中外合作 Sino-foreign Contractual Joint Ventures	107	96	99	88	88	66	74	86	82	83	87
中外合资 Sino-foreign Equity Joint Ventures	1 092	1 184	1 356	1 549	1 818	1 586	2 095	2 561	2 748	2 842	2 858
外商独资 Foreign Investment Enterprises	2 046	2 595	3 270	3 957	4 294	3 799	5 212	6 002	5 883	5 823	6 149
集体企业/私营企业 Collective Enterprises/Private owned Enterprises	177	205	200	232	289	265	349	407	353	4 368	4 475
其他 Other Enterprises	427	549	738	1 035	1 304	1 454	2 343	3 445	4 158	1 397	1 124
出口 Export	**5 934**	**7 620**	**9 691**	**12 180**	**14 285**	**12 017**	**15 779**	**18 986**	**20 489**	**22 100**	**23 427**
国有企业 State-owned Enterprises	1 536	1 688	1 913	2 248	2 572	1 910	2 344	2 672	2 563	2 490	2 565
外商投资企业 Foreign-funded Enterprises	3 386	4 442	5 638	6 955	7 906	6 722	8 623	9 953	10 227	10 443	10 747
中外合作 Sino-foreign Contractual Joint Ventures	148	157	177	181	183	146	165	177	162	157	136
中外合资 Sino-foreign Equity Joint Ventures	1 096	1 360	1 638	1 988	2 269	1 824	2 376	2 731	2 873	3 009	3 055
外商独资 Foreign Investment Enterprises	2 142	2 925	3 824	4 786	5 454	4 752	6 082	7 046	7 193	7 277	7 556
集体企业/私营企业 Collective Enterprises/Private owned Enterprises	318	365	411	469	547	405	499	554	509	8 633	9 547
其他 Other Enterprises	694	1 125	1 728	2 508	3 260	2 979	4 314	5 807	7 190	534	958
差额 Balance	**319**	**1 019**	**1 775**	**2 622**	**2 955**	**1 961**	**1 831**	**1 551**	**2 311**	**2 598**	**3 825**
国有企业 State-owned Enterprises	−229	−284	−339	−449	−966	−975	−1 532	−2 262	−2 391	−2 500	−2 346
外商投资企业 Foreign-funded Enterprises	140	567	912	1 361	1 706	1 270	1 243	1 305	1 515	1 695	1 654
中外合作 Sino-foreign Contractual Joint Ventures	40	61	78	93	95	80	91	91	80	74	49
中外合资 Sino-foreign Equity Joint Ventures	4	176	281	439	451	238	281	170	125	167	197
外商独资 Foreign Investment Enterprises	96	330	553	829	1 160	953	870	1 044	1 310	1 454	1 407
集体企业/私营企业 Collective Enterprises/Private owned Enterprises	141	160	211	237	258	140	150	147	156	4 265	5 072
其他 Other Enterprises	267	576	990	1 473	1 956	1 525	1 971	2 362	3 032	−863	−166

注：2013年集体企业项下的数据由集体企业调整为私营企业。
Note: Data of Collective Enterprises was replaced by that of Private Owned Enterprises from 2013.

2014 年按贸易方式分类的进口构成
Components of Import by Trading Forms in 2014

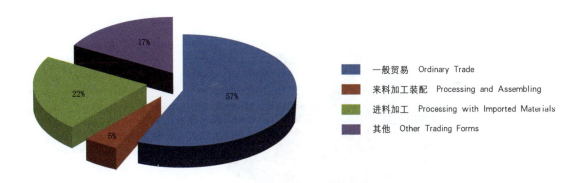

- 一般贸易 Ordinary Trade
- 来料加工装配 Processing and Assembling
- 进料加工 Processing with Imported Materials
- 其他 Other Trading Forms

2014 年按贸易方式分类的出口构成
Components of Export by Trading Forms in 2014

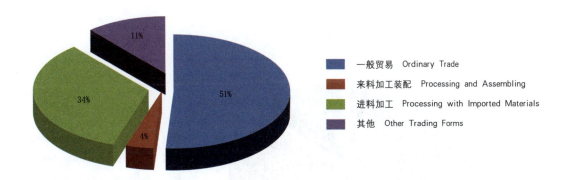

- 一般贸易 Ordinary Trade
- 来料加工装配 Processing and Assembling
- 进料加工 Processing with Imported Materials
- 其他 Other Trading Forms

2014 年按企业类型分类的进口构成
Components of Import by Type of Enterprises in 2014

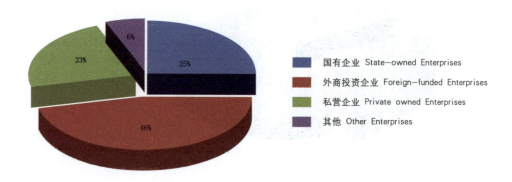

- 国有企业 State—owned Enterprises
- 外商投资企业 Foreign—funded Enterprises
- 私营企业 Private owned Enterprises
- 其他 Other Enterprises

2014 年按企业类型分类的出口构成
Components of Export by Type of Enterprises in 2014

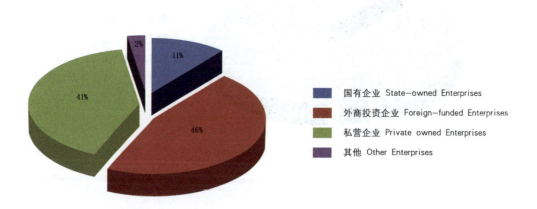

- 国有企业 State—owned Enterprises
- 外商投资企业 Foreign—funded Enterprises
- 私营企业 Private owned Enterprises
- 其他 Other Enterprises

2014年进出口按贸易方式分类

单位：亿美元
Unit: USD 100 million

Import & Export by Trading Forms in 2014

贸易方式 Trading Forms	进口 Import		出口 Export		进出口差额 Import & Export Balance
	金额Value	同比（%）Increase	金额Value	同比（%）Increase	
总值 Total Value	**19 603**	**0.5**	**23 427**	**6.1**	**3 825**
一般贸易 Ordinary Trade	11 095	0.0	12 037	10.7	942
加工贸易 Processing Trade	5 244	5.5	8 844	2.7	3 600
来料加工装配 Processing and Assembling	975	11.5	907	−1.9	−68
进料加工 Processing with imported materials	4 268	4.2	7 937	3.4	3 669
其他贸易 Other trading forms	3 264	−5.0	2 546	−2.7	−718

2014年进出口按企业类型分类

单位：亿美元
Unit: USD 100 million

Import & Export by Type of Enterprises in 2014

企业类型　Type of Enterprises	进口　Import		出口　Export		进出口差额 Import & Export Balance
	金额Value	同比（%）Increase	金额Value	同比（%）Increase	
总值 **Total Value**	**19 603**	**0.5**	**2 3427**	**6.1**	**3 825**
国有企业 State-owned Enterprises	4 911	−1.9	2 565	3.1	−2 346
外资企业 Ｆｏｒｅｉｇｎ-ｆｕｎｄｅｄ Enterprises	9 093	3.9	10 747	3.0	1 654
私营和其他企业 Private Owned and other Enterprises	5 599	−2.9	10 115	10.3	4 516

2014 年前十位贸易伙伴（按进出口总值）

Top 10 Trading Partners in 2014
(Based on the Total Value of Import & Export)

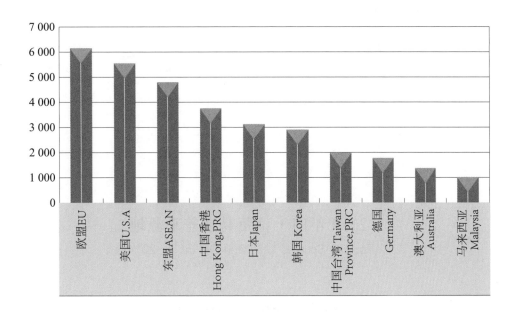

亿美元
USD 100 million

2014 年前十位贸易顺差来源地

Top 10 Sources of Trade Surplus in 2014

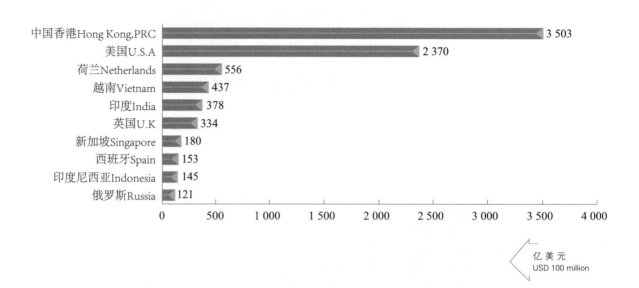

2014 年前十位贸易逆差来源地

Top 10 Sources of Trade Deficit in 2014

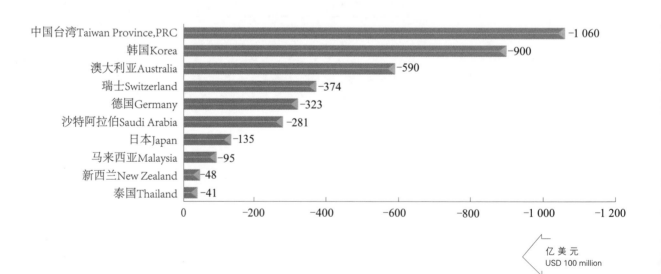

三、外汇市场和人民币汇率[①]

Ⅲ. Foreign Exchange Market and Exchange Rate of RMB

人民币对美元交易中间价月平均汇价

人民币元/100美元
RMB per 100 USD

Monthly Average Transaction Mid Rates of Pemininbi against US, 1980—2014

月份Month \ 年份year	1980	1981	1982	1983	1984	1985	1986	1987	1988	1989	1990
1 月/Jan.	149.37	154.87	176.77	192.01	204.12	280.88	320.15	372.21	372.21	372.21	472.21
2 月/Feb.	150.05	161.06	181.74	196.03	205.72	282.51	320.70	372.21	372.21	372.21	472.21
3 月/Mar.	155.12	162.80	183.79	197.80	206.08	284.51	321.20	372.21	372.21	372.21	472.21
4 月/Apr.	155.70	166.20	185.19	198.72	208.91	284.11	320.61	372.21	372.21	372.21	472.21
5 月/May	149.06	172.27	180.97	198.52	218.21	284.75	319.44	372.21	372.21	372.21	472.21
6 月/Jun.	146.50	176.05	189.70	198.95	221.22	286.25	320.35	372.21	372.21	372.21	472.21
7 月/Jul.	145.25	175.98	192.36	198.88	229.39	287.38	363.82	372.21	372.21	372.21	472.21
8 月/Aug.	147.26	179.52	193.87	198.00	236.43	290.23	370.36	372.21	372.21	372.21	472.21
9 月/Sept.	146.81	175.01	195.04	198.14	253.26	296.26	370.66	372.21	372.21	372.21	472.21
10 月/Oct.	148.03	175.05	198.22	196.17	264.00	306.73	371.64	372.21	372.21	372.21	472.21
11月/Nov.	151.73	173.46	199.41	198.90	266.16	320.15	372.21	372.21	372.21	372.21	495.54
12月/Dec.	154.19	173.78	193.99	198.69	278.91	320.15	372.21	372.21	372.21	423.82	522.21
年平均 Annual Average	149.84	170.50	189.25	197.57	232.70	293.66	345.28	372.21	372.21	376.51	478.32

①资料来源：国家外汇管理局相关资料。
Source：State Administration of Foreign Exchange.

人民币对美元交易中间价月平均汇价

人民币元/100美元
RMB per 100 USD

Monthly Average Transaction Mid Rates of RMB against USD, 1980—2014

月份Month ＼ 年份year	1991	1992	1993	1994	1995	1996	1997	1998	1999	2000	2001
1 月/Jan.	522.21	544.81	576.40	870.00	844.13	831.86	829.63	827.91	827.90	827.93	827.71
2 月/Feb.	522.21	546.35	576.99	870.28	843.54	831.32	829.29	827.91	827.80	827.79	827.70
3 月/Mar.	522.21	547.34	573.13	870.23	842.76	832.89	829.57	827.92	827.91	827.86	827.76
4 月/Apr.	526.59	549.65	570.63	869.55	842.25	833.15	829.57	827.92	827.92	827.93	827.71
5 月/May	531.39	550.36	572.17	866.49	831.28	832.88	829.29	827.90	827.85	827.77	827.72
6 月/Jun.	535.35	547.51	573.74	865.72	830.08	832.26	829.21	827.97	827.80	827.72	827.71
7 月/Jul.	535.55	544.32	576.12	864.03	830.07	831.60	829.11	827.98	827.77	827.93	827.69
8 月/Aug.	537.35	542.87	577.64	858.98	830.75	830.81	828.94	827.99	827.73	827.96	827.70
9 月/Sept.	537.35	549.48	578.70	854.03	831.88	830.44	828.72	827.89	827.74	827.86	827.68
10 月/Oct.	537.90	553.69	578.68	852.93	831.55	830.00	828.38	827.78	827.74	827.85	827.68
11月/Nov.	538.58	561.31	579.47	851.69	831.35	829.93	828.11	827.78	827.82	827.74	827.69
12月/Dec.	541.31	579.82	580.68	848.45	831.56	829.90	827.96	827.79	827.93	827.72	827.68
年平均 Annual Average	532.33	551.46	576.20	861.87	835.10	831.42	828.98	827.91	827.83	827.84	827.70

人民币对美元交易中间价月平均汇价

人民币元/100美元
RMB per 100 USD

Monthly Average Transaction Mid Rates of RMB against USD, 1980—2014

月份Month \ 年份year	2002	2003	2004	2005	2006	2007	2008	2009	2010	2011	2012	2013	2014
1 月/Jan.	827.67	827.68	827.69	827.65	806.68	778.98	724.78	683.82	682.73	660.27	631.68	627.87	610.43
2 月/Feb.	827.66	827.73	827.71	827.65	804.93	775.46	716.01	683.57	682.70	658.31	630.00	628.42	611.28
3 月/Mar.	827.70	827.72	827.71	827.65	803.50	773.90	707.52	683.41	682.64	656.62	630.81	627.43	613.58
4 月/Apr.	827.72	827.71	827.69	827.65	801.56	772.47	700.07	683.12	682.62	652.92	629.66	624.71	615.53
5 月/May	827.69	827.69	827.71	827.65	801.52	767.04	697.24	682.45	682.74	649.88	630.62	619.70	616.36
6 月/Jun.	827.70	827.71	827.67	827.65	800.67	763.30	689.71	683.32	681.65	647.78	631.78	617.18	615.57
7 月/Jul.	827.68	827.73	827.67	822.90	799.10	758.05	683.76	683.20	677.75	646.14	632.35	617.25	615.69
8 月/Aug.	827.67	827.70	827.68	810.19	797.33	757.53	685.15	683.22	679.01	640.9	634.04	617.08	616.06
9 月/Sept.	827.70	827.71	827.67	809.22	793.68	752.58	683.07	682.89	674.62	638.33	633.95	615.88	615.28
10 月/Oct.	827.69	827.67	827.65	808.89	790.32	750.12	683.16	682.75	667.32	635.66	631.44	613.93	614.41
11月/Nov.	827.71	827.69	827.65	808.40	786.52	742.33	682.86	682.74	665.58	634.08	629.53	613.72	614.32
12月/Dec.	827.72	827.70	827.65	807.59	782.38	736.76	684.24	682.79	665.15	632.81	629.00	611.60	612.38
年平均 Annual Average	827.70	827.70	827.68	819.42	797.18	760.40	694.51	683.10	676.95	646.14	631.25	619.32	614.28

2014年1~12月人民币市场汇率汇总表

林吉特、卢布单位：外币/100元人民币
其他9种币种单位：人民币元/100外币
MYR, RUB Unit: foreign currency per 100 RMB
Other 9 Currency unit: RMB per 100 foreign currency

Transaction Mid Rates of RMB in 2014

月份Month	币种 Currency	期初价 Beginning of Period	期末价 End of Period	最高价 Highest	最低价 Lowest	期平均 Period Average	累计平均 Accumulative Average
1月 Jan.	美元USD	609.90	610.50	611.09	609.30	610.43	610.43
	港元HKD	78.658	78.625	78.806	78.575	78.694	78.694
	日元JPY	5.7827	5.9625	5.9625	5.7827	5.8544	5.8544
	欧元EUR	839.37	833.88	839.37	825.57	831.79	831.79
	英镑GBP	1 011.18	1 010.87	1 014.74	997.78	1 005.34	1 005.34
	澳元AUD	542.12	531.38	549.81	529.49	540.03	540.03
	加元CAD	573.21	546.14	574.86	546.14	559.19	559.19
	林吉特MYR	53.976	55.037	55.077	53.602	54.340	54.340
	卢布RUB	541.34	577.91	577.91	541.34	554.53	554.53
2月 Feb.	美元USD	610.89	612.14	612.24	610.53	611.28	610.79
	港元HKD	78.733	78.878	78.893	78.722	78.801	78.740
	日元JPY	5.9732	6.0022	6.0022	5.9358	5.9641	5.9019
	欧元EUR	830.05	838.97	841.05	830.05	836.75	833.93
	英镑GBP	997.06	1 021.36	1 023.13	997.06	1 015.08	1 009.55
	澳元AUD	546.07	548.45	552.22	545.67	548.82	543.83
	加元CAD	551.94	549.97	557.74	549.83	553.18	556.59
	林吉特MYR	54.517	53.501	54.930	53.501	54.216	54.287
	卢布RUB	571.89	588.13	588.13	568.08	579.44	565.30
3月 Mar.	美元USD	611.90	615.21	615.21	611.90	613.58	611.80
	港元HKD	78.836	79.305	79.305	78.836	79.054	78.854
	日元JPY	6.0391	5.9920	6.0562	5.9333	6.0057	5.9394
	欧元EUR	843.05	846.07	854.63	841.01	848.26	839.12
	英镑GBP	1 023.83	1 023.83	1 026.00	1 013.22	1 019.76	1 013.24
	澳元AUD	544.55	569.65	571.78	544.55	556.80	548.53
	加元CAD	553.15	556.83	557.63	546.31	552.30	555.04
	林吉特MYR	53.631	52.757	53.631	52.757	53.357	53.950
	卢布RUB	587.12	576.87	596.20	573.59	587.10	573.19
4月 Apr.	美元USD	615.03	615.80	616.10	614.90	615.53	612.79
	港元HKD	79.285	79.425	79.457	79.272	79.378	78.993
	日元JPY	5.9761	6.0235	6.0749	5.9376	6.0202	5.9609
	欧元EUR	847.11	850.33	854.38	844.65	850.01	842.02
	英镑GBP	1 024.70	1 036.02	1 036.62	1 021.54	1 030.80	1 017.91
	澳元AUD	571.79	573.07	581.21	569.04	574.68	555.48
	新西兰元NZD	534.75	529.27	537.58	527.51	531.44	531.44
	加元CAD	556.51	562.22	565.56	556.51	559.67	556.27
	林吉特MYR	52.735	52.502	53.046	52.062	52.556	53.580
	卢布RUB	566.14	571.58	583.58	565.95	574.51	573.54

2014年1~12月人民币市场汇率汇总表

林吉特、卢布单位：外币/100元人民币
其他9种币种单位：人民币元/100外币
MYR, RUB Unit: foreign currency per 100 RMB
Other 9 Currency unit: RMB per 100 foreign currency

Transaction Mid Rates of RMB in 2014

月份Month	币种 Currency	期初价 Beginning of Period	期末价 End of Period	最高价 Highest	最低价 Lowest	期平均 Period Average	累计平均 Accumulative Average
5月 May.	美元USD	615.60	616.95	617.05	615.42	616.36	613.51
	港元HKD	79.404	79.578	79.587	79.389	79.505	79.097
	日元JPY	6.0495	6.0903	6.1008	6.0445	6.0726	5.9835
	欧元EUR	853.74	839.21	857.56	839.10	846.37	842.90
	英镑GBP	1 038.89	1 031.88	1 044.98	1 031.58	1 038.26	1 022.02
	澳元AUD	573.10	576.03	578.80	570.02	574.76	559.38
	新西兰元NZD	535.08	524.94	536.67	524.94	531.75	531.59
	加元CAD	560.86	569.30	569.30	560.86	566.07	558.25
	林吉特MYR	52.572	51.639	52.572	51.495	52.009	53.262
	卢布RUB	574.71	556.85	574.71	542.12	559.40	570.68
6月 Jun.	美元USD	617.10	615.28	617.10	614.51	615.57	613.86
	港元HKD	79.588	79.375	79.593	79.274	79.410	79.149
	日元JPY	6.0450	6.0815	6.0815	6.0214	6.0467	5.9941
	欧元EUR	839.41	839.46	841.86	832.27	836.87	841.88
	英镑GBP	1 033.70	1 049.78	1 050.42	1 030.01	1 041.61	1 025.31
	澳元AUD	571.70	580.64	581.04	571.70	577.74	562.46
	新西兰元NZD	522.86	541.03	541.29	521.57	532.19	531.79
	加元CAD	566.20	576.86	576.86	562.15	568.23	559.93
	林吉特MYR	51.978	51.906	52.137	51.537	51.926	53.038
	卢布RUB	561.84	544.10	570.72	542.61	553.87	567.86
7月 Jul.	美元USD	615.23	616.75	616.75	614.43	615.69	614.16
	港元HKD	79.381	79.581	79.581	79.281	79.440	79.196
	日元JPY	6.0778	6.0012	6.0922	6.0012	6.0652	6.0056
	欧元EUR	842.34	826.23	842.34	826.23	834.25	840.65
	英镑GBP	1 053.91	1 043.71	1 059.04	1 043.71	1 053.45	1 029.87
	澳元AUD	580.17	575.33	587.99	575.33	579.40	565.21
	新西兰元NZD	539.75	523.92	543.61	523.92	536.19	532.99
	加元CAD	576.38	565.49	579.51	565.49	573.98	562.20
	林吉特MYR	51.873	51.613	51.873	51.260	51.512	52.791
	卢布RUB	549.04	576.28	577.84	548.46	560.37	566.65
8月 Agu.	美元USD	616.81	616.47	616.81	615.17	616.06	614.40
	港元HKD	79.588	79.543	79.588	79.366	79.487	79.234
	日元JPY	6.0026	5.9396	6.0393	5.9168	5.9850	6.0030
	欧元EUR	825.88	812.60	827.95	811.20	820.62	838.07
	英镑GBP	1 042.03	1 021.89	1 042.03	1 019.82	1 029.63	1 029.84
	澳元AUD	574.13	575.88	576.52	569.50	573.19	566.23
	新西兰元NZD	524.83	515.78	525.61	512.96	519.37	530.27
	加元CAD	565.47	567.76	567.78	560.72	563.87	562.42
	林吉特MYR	51.851	51.307	52.120	51.087	51.617	52.639
	卢布RUB	579.09	597.45	597.45	579.09	585.66	569.09

2014年1～12月人民币市场汇率汇总表

林吉特、卢布单位：外币/100元人民币
其他9种币种单位：人民币元/100外币
MYR, RUB Unit: foreign currency per 100 RMB
Other 9 Currency unit: RMB per 100 foreign currency

Transaction Mid Rates of RMB in 2014

月份Month	币种 Currency	期初价 Beginning of Period	期末价 End of Period	最高价 Highest	最低价 Lowest	期平均 Period Average	累计平均 Accumulative Average
9月 Sep.	美元USD	616.80	615.25	617.07	614.25	615.28	614.50
	港元HKD	79.584	79.246	79.619	79.246	79.371	79.249
	日元JPY	5.9157	5.6242	5.9157	5.6242	5.7381	5.9727
	欧元EUR	809.58	780.49	810.75	780.49	794.66	833.11
	英镑GBP	1 022.51	998.77	1 023.58	991.74	1 004.25	1 026.92
	澳元AUD	574.99	535.61	576.16	535.61	557.20	565.20
	新西兰元NZD	515.11	476.93	516.41	476.93	501.73	525.51
	加元CAD	567.09	550.98	567.57	550.98	559.31	562.06
	林吉特MYR	51.181	52.983	53.188	51.181	52.287	52.599
	卢布RUB	601.98	641.01	641.01	599.45	617.33	574.60
10月 Oct.	美元USD	614.93	614.61	614.93	613.95	614.41	614.49
	港元HKD	79.297	79.252	79.297	79.150	79.209	79.246
	日元JPY	5.6840	5.6162	5.7912	5.6162	5.7079	5.9491
	欧元EUR	778.12	773.77	787.49	773.66	779.92	828.37
	英镑GBP	988.67	982.02	993.14	976.05	986.86	1 023.35
	澳元AUD	541.70	541.60	543.64	533.62	539.06	562.87
	新西兰元NZD	480.67	480.68	489.42	478.45	483.87	520.31
	新加坡元SGD	481.84	480.57	482.25	480.40	481.27	481.27
	加元CAD	550.82	548.86	553.50	542.77	547.46	560.76
	林吉特MYR	53.043	53.655	53.655	52.915	53.268	52.659
	卢布RUB	650.10	678.51	703.77	650.10	670.42	583.14
11月 Nov.	美元USD	615.25	613.45	616.02	613.20	614.32	614.48
	港元HKD	79.331	79.126	79.454	79.080	79.223	79.244
	日元JPY	5.4474	5.1937	5.4474	5.1937	5.2882	5.8896
	欧元EUR	766.96	764.08	770.66	760.39	765.99	822.75
	英镑GBP	979.98	964.11	982.72	958.28	969.20	1 018.47
	澳元AUD	536.35	522.48	537.51	522.48	531.04	560.01
	新西兰元NZD	476.95	481.79	487.45	472.83	480.58	515.46
	新加坡元SGD	477.26	471.58	477.26	471.19	474.01	475.22
	加元CAD	544.71	540.39	546.98	539.12	542.27	559.10
	林吉特MYR	53.821	54.797	54.797	53.821	54.495	52.824
	卢布RUB	702.07	792.05	792.05	702.07	750.37	598.20
12月 Dec.	美元USD	613.69	611.90	614.11	611.37	612.38	614.28
	港元HKD	79.139	78.887	79.206	78.844	78.967	79.218
	日元JPY	5.1938	5.1371	5.2455	5.0545	5.1436	5.8196
	欧元EUR	763.35	745.56	766.12	745.56	756.21	816.51
	英镑GBP	958.07	954.37	965.35	952.50	959.23	1 012.91
	澳元AUD	518.71	501.74	520.67	497.67	505.96	554.93
	新西兰元NZD	478.58	480.34	482.78	468.77	476.06	510.62
	新加坡元SGD	469.13	463.96	471.65	463.71	466.46	470.93
	加元CAD	535.74	527.55	541.41	524.85	530.77	556.44
	林吉特MYR	55.604	56.737	56.878	55.604	56.486	53.168
	卢布RUB	820.30	905.36	1 134.33	820.30	911.39	627.60

1979-2014 年人民币对美元交易中间价月平均汇价

Monthly Average Transaction Mid Rates of RMB Against USD, 1979-2014

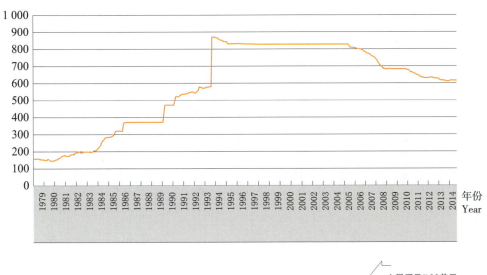

人民币元/100美元
RMB per 100 USD

四、利用外资①

IV. Foreign Investment Utilization

外商直接投资

Foreign Direct Investment

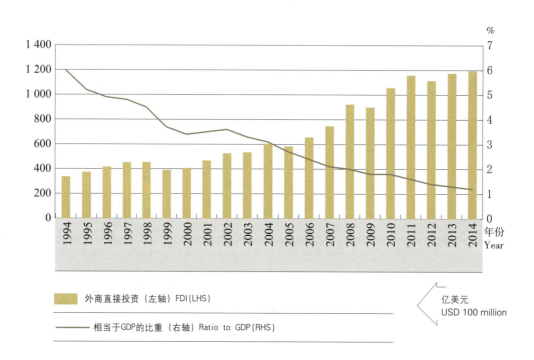

外商直接投资（左轴）FDI(LHS)

相当于GDP的比重（右轴）Ratio to GDP(RHS)

亿美元
USD 100 million

①资料来源：商务部。
Source: Ministry of Commerce.

2014年利用外资

Foreign Direct Investment in 2014

单位：亿美元
Unit: USD 100 million

利用外资方式 Mode of Foreign Investment Utilization	本年批准外资项目数 Approved Foreign Investment Programs		本年实际使用外资 Actual Utilization of Foreign Investment	
	本年累计 Accumulative in This Year	同比增长(%) Increase	本年累计 Accumulative in This Year	同比增长(%) Increase
总计 Total	**23 778**	**4.4**	**1 197.1**	**0.8**
一、外商直接投资 Direct Foreign Investment	23 778	4.4	1 195.6	1.7
中外合资企业 Sino-Foreign Equity Joint Venture	4824	7.8	210.0	−11.7
中外合作企业 Sino-Foreign Contractual Joint Venture	104	−26.8	16.3	−16
外资企业 Foreign Investment Enterprise	18 809	3.8	947.4	5.8
外商投资股份制 Stock-Holding by Foreign Investment	41	36.67	21.9	−4.0
合作开发 Cooperation Exploitation	0	0	0	0
其他 Others	0	0	0	0
二、外商其他投资 Other Foreign Investment	0	0	1.4	−87.3
对外发行股票 Issue Stocks to the Outside	0	0	0	0
国际租赁 International Tenancy	0	0	0	0
补偿贸易 Compensative Trade	0	0	0	0
加工装配 Processing & Assembling	0	0	1.4	−82.2

注：统计数据为非金融领域。
Notes：The data is subject to non-financial sectors.

五、外债[①]

V. External Debt

外债余额

External Debt

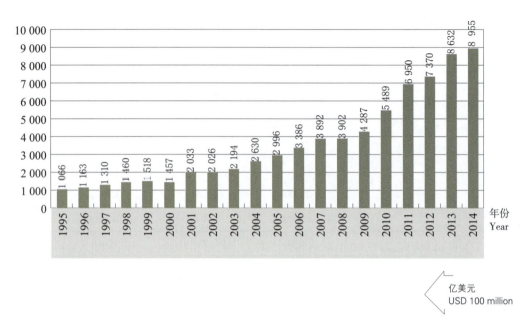

亿美元
USD 100 million

外债余额期限结构（剩余期限）

Components of External Debt by Period Structure（Residual Maturity）

■ 中长期外债余额Long-and-Medium-term External Debt

■ 短期外债余额Short-term External Debt

亿美元
USD 100 million

① 数据来源：国家外汇管理局。
Sources: State Administration of Foreign Exchange.

2014 年末外债余额期限结构（剩余期限）
Components of External Debt by Period Structure (Residual Maturity), End—2014

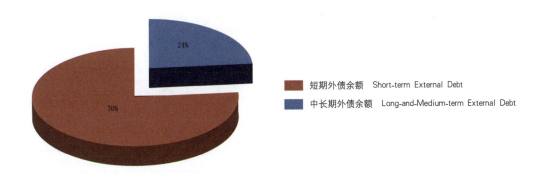

24%

76%

■ 短期外债余额　Short-term External Debt
■ 中长期外债余额　Long-and-Medium-term External Debt

2014 年末登记外债余额主体结构
Components of Registered External Debt by Type of Debtor, End—2014

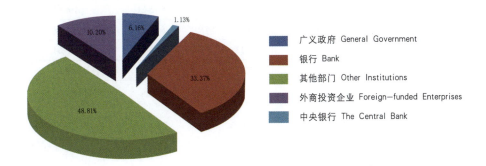

1.13%

6.16%

10.20%

33.37%

48.81%

■ 广义政府 General Government
■ 银行 Bank
■ 其他部门 Other Institutions
■ 外商投资企业 Foreign—funded Enterprises
■ 中央银行 The Central Bank

六、国际旅游[①]

VI. International Tourism

入境过夜旅游者人数和旅游外汇收入

Number of Inbound Stay—over Tourists and Foreign Exchange Income from Tourism

年份 Year	入境过夜旅游（万人次） Inbound Stay-over Tourists(10 000 persons)	旅游外汇收入（亿美元） Foreign Exchange Income from Tourism(USD 100 million)	年份 Year	入境过夜旅游（万人次） Inbound Stay-over Tourists(10 000 persons)	旅游外汇收入（亿美元） Foreign Exchange Income from Tourism(USD 100 million)
1978	71.6	2.63	1996	2 276.5	102.00
1979	152.9	4.49	1997	2 377.0	120.74
1980	350.0	6.17	1998	2 507.3	126.02
1981	367.7	7.85	1999	2 704.7	140.99
1982	392.4	8.43	2000	3 122.9	162.24
1983	379.1	9.41	2001	3 316.7	177.92
1984	514.1	11.31	2002	3 680.3	203.85
1985	713.3	12.50	2003	3 297.1	174.06
1986	900.1	15.31	2004	4 176.1	257.39
1987	1 076.0	18.62	2005	4 680.9	292.96
1988	1 236.1	22.47	2006	4 991.0	339.49
1989	936.1	18.60	2007	5 472.0	419.19
1990	1 048.4	22.18	2008	5 304.9	408.43
1991	1 246.4	28.45	2009	5 087.5	396.75
1992	1 651.2	39.47	2010	5 566.5	458.14
1993	1 898.2	46.83	2011	5 758.1	484.64
1994	2 107.0	73.23	2012	5 772.5	500.28
1995	2 003.4	87.33	2013	5 568.6	516.64
			2014	5 562.2	569.13

①资料来源：国家旅游局。
Soicrce：China National Tourism Administration.

七、世界经济增长状况[①]

VII. Growth of World Economics

世界主要经济体增长率
Growth Rate of Major Economies in the World

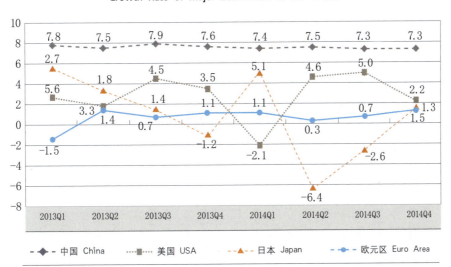

经济增长率 (%)
Growth Rate of Economy (%)

世界主要经济体通货膨胀水平
Inflation Rate of Major Economies in the World

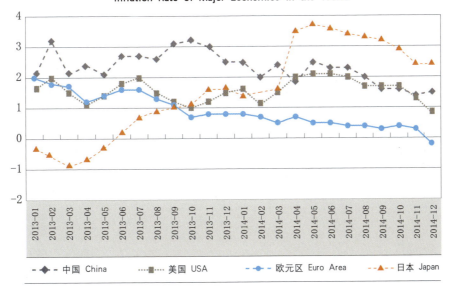

居民消费价格指数
CPI（%）

①资料来源：彭博资讯；CEIC Asia Database.
Sources：Bloomberg，CEIC Asia Database.

世界主要经济体就业状况
Employment of Major Economies in the World

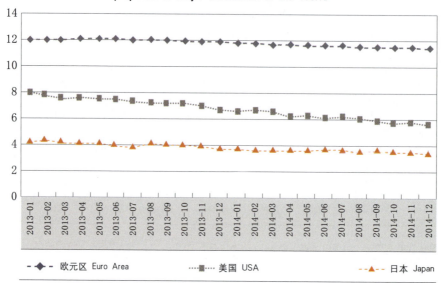

欧元区 Euro Area　　　　美国 USA　　　　日本 Japan

失业率 (%)
Unemployment Rate (%)

八、国际金融市场状况^①

Ⅷ. International Financial Market

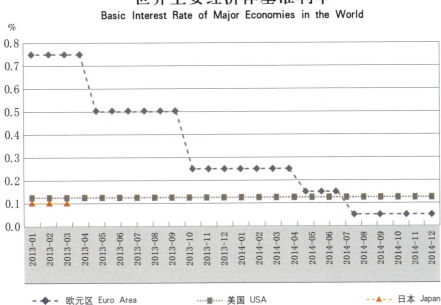

世界主要经济体基准利率
Basic Interest Rate of Major Economies in the World

美国、德国及日本股票指数走势
The trend of stock indices in the markets of U.S.A, Germany and Japan

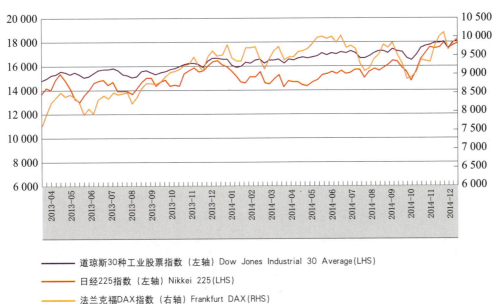

① 资料来源：彭博资讯。
Sources：Bloomberg.

国际商品价格
Price of International Commodities

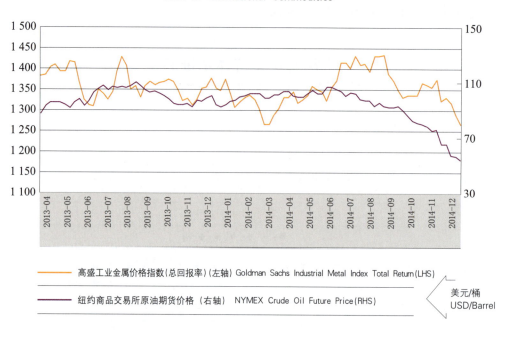

高盛工业金属价格指数（总回报率）（左轴）Goldman Sachs Industrial Metal Index Total Return（LHS）

纽约商品交易所原油期货价格（右轴） NYMEX Crude Oil Future Price（RHS）

美元/桶
USD/Barrel

伦敦金属交易所金银价格
LME Gold and Silver Price

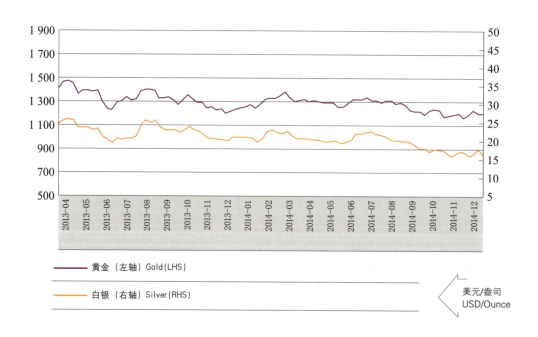

黄金（左轴）Gold（LHS）

白银（右轴）Silver（RHS）

美元/盎司
USD/Ounce